SEMINOLE

OF

FLORIDA

INDIAN CENSUS 1930-1940
WITH
BIRTH AND DEATH RECORDS
1930-1938

I0209918

TRANSCRIBED BY
JEFF BOWEN

NATIVE STUDY
Gallipolis, Ohio
USA

Originally published:
Baltimore, Maryland
2011

Reprinted by:

Native Study LLC
Gallipolis, OH
www.nativestudy.com

Library of Congress Control Number: 2020911440

ISBN: 978-1-64968-000-6

Made in the United States of America.

Table of Contents

INTRODUCTION

In 1819, Andrew Jackson inaugurated a forceful policy of tribal removal to open the land for white settlers. Resistance by the tribe led to the Seminole Wars. Their leader, Osceola, headed the fight to protect these lands. After his capture in 1837, and the end of the Second Seminole War in 1842, thousands of Seminoles were vigorously moved west to Indian Territory (present Oklahoma), where they were settled in the western part of the Creek reservation. In 1858, the Third Seminole War ended and 250 more were sent west. In 1970, the Indian Claims Commission awarded the Seminoles $12 million for the lands they lost as a result of these three wars. A few Seminoles remained in Florida, where their descendants numbered about 12,797 in 1990.

The information in this book was taken from Archival film Series M595, Roll #487, NATIVE AMERICAN, CENSUS ROLLS, 1885-1940; Seminole (Florida): 1930-40. You will notice as you look through the book that some census years are missing or incomplete. In numerous places rather than recording a person's name the word: Unknown" was used. Comparisons to other census numbers with other years were used to match a name with a census number for verification in some situations, but in many cases, the problem of the word "Unknown" couldn't be overcome. It was felt as though there was still too much important information to be sought from this piece of work to allow it to go unfinished.

The names are, for the most part, arranged in alphabetical order. However, there were several names associated with family listings that were not listed in alphabetical order. These names have been listed on a limited index in the back of the book. In some cases you will notice family members names are bolded, this is because their names are different than the Head of Household.

Jeff Bowen
Gallipolis, Ohio
Nativestudy.com

(*A*) A separate roll is to be made of each reservation; also, of each *rancheria* or reserve, and a separate roll of Indians allotted on the public domain or homesteading. The roll is to be based on enrollment and not on residence.

(*B*) Persons are to be listed by families alphabetically; that is, not only by the first letter of the surname, but also by the second and subsequent letters when the first letter or letters are the same. For example: Ab*a*lon, Ab*b*ott, Ab*c*on, Ab*e*nd, Ab*i*ct; B*a*ll, B*e*ll, B*i*ll, B*o*ll, B*u*ll; ...etc. Families having the same surname are also to be listed in this way, e.g.; Brown, *A*nson; Brown, *B*ill; Brown, *C*harles; Brown, *D*avid. In the case of English translations of Indian names, such as John *Flying-Elk*, Flying-Elk is the surname and is to be listed under F. In such cases the first word of the translated Indian name determines the alphabetical position. The best way to accomplish this will be to write the names of each family group on a separate card; then, arrange the cards alphabetically and type the names therefrom onto the census roll.

Members of a family are to be listed in the following order: Head, first; wife, second; then children, whether sons or daughters, *in the order of their ages*; and lastly, all other relatives and persons living with the family who do not constitute another family group.

Annuity and per capita payment rolls are also to be prepared in the same manner.

(*C*) A family is composed of the following members:
      1. Both parents and their unmarried children, if any, living with them; all other relatives and persons living with the family who do not constitute another family group.
      2. Either parent and the unmarried children, if the other parent is dead; all other relatives and persons living with the family who do not constitute another family group.
      3. A single person over 21 years of age, not living with a relative.

(*D*) For each person the following information is to be furnished:
      1. NUMBER. – A number is to be assigned in serial order. Thus, the first person listed is to be numbered as "1," the second, as "2," and so on until the census is completed.
      2. NAME. – If there are both an Indian and an English name, the allotment or annuity roll name

is to be given. First, the last or surname;
then, the given name in full. Ditto marks
are to be used under the surname of the
head for the surnames of the other
members of one family.

3. SEX. – "M" for male; "F" for female.
4. AGE AT LAST BIRTHDAY. – Age in completed years
      at last birthday is to be shown. For
infants under 1 year, age in completed
months, expressed as twelfths of a year.
Thus, 3 months as 3/12 yr.

5. TRIBE. – Care is to be taken that tribe, not bank or
      local name, is given. Thus, Ute tribe, not
Pahvant, which is a band of Ute.
Likewise, Hupa tribe, not Bear River,
which is a local name for the members of
the Hupa tribe living near Bear River.

6. DEGREE OF BLOOD. – "F" for full blood; "1/4+" for
      one-fourth or more Indian blood; "-1/4"
for less than one fourth Indian blood.

7. MARITAL STATUS. – "S" for a single or unmarried
      person; "M" for a married person; and
"W" for widowed of either sex.

8. RELATIONSHIP TO HEAD OF FAMILY. – The
      head, whether husband or father, widow
or unmarried person of either sex, is to be
designated as such. For the other
members, the appropriate term which
designates the particular relationship the
person bears to the head is to be used.

9. RESIDENCE. –

      (*a*) At *jurisdiction* where enrolled: Yes or no.
      The term jurisdiction includes all
reservations and public domain
allotments under the agency.

      (*b*) *Or* at another jurisdiction. The name of the
      jurisdiction is to be given.

      (*c*) *Or* elsewhere:

            1. Post office: Both the proper name of
            the post office and the class by which it is

known (city, town, village, etc.) are to be given. Thus, Lewiston, city.
2. County.
3. State.

10. WARD. – Yes or no. Wardship depends primarily upon the ownership of individual property held in trust or upon membership in a tribe living on a Federal reservation.

11. ALLOTMENT, ANNUITY, AND IDENTIFICATION NUMBERS.—"Al", for allotment; "An", for annuity; and "Id". for identification, before the appropriate number or numbers. All numbers are to be shown.

(*E*) Rolls not prepared in strict conformity with the above instructions will be returned for correction.

Florida Seminoles Indian Census (As of April 1, 1930)

KEY: Census Number Name Sex Age at Last Birthday Tribe (Seminole, unless otherwise stated) Degree of Blood Marital Status Relationship to Head of Family At Jurisdiction where enrolled [Yes or No] (If no, Where) Ward [Yes or No] Allotment, Annuity, and Identification Numbers (if given).

BILLIE

1	Mrs. Carney f 30 F w Head yes no
2	Unknown f 13 F s dau yes no
3	Unknown m 11 F s son yes no
4	Unknown m 9 F s son yes no
5	Unknown f 7 F s dau yes no
6	Unknown m 5 F s son yes no
7	Unknown f 3 F s dau yes no
8	Rosalie f 16 F s sister yes no

9	Charley m 50 F m Head yes no
10	Mona f 46 F m wife yes no
11	Chestnut m 24 F s son yes no
12	Ruby f 22 F s dau yes no
13	Maggie f 18 F s dau yes no

| 14 | Cowboy m 20 F m Head yes no |
| 15 | Annie f 14 F m wife yes no |

| 16 | Girtman m 34 F w Head yes no |
| 17 | To-hi-kee m 12 F s son yes no |

18	Kunzie m 34 F m Head yes no
19	Addie f 31 F m wife yes no
20	Unknown m 8 F s son yes no
21	Unknown f 12 F s dau yes no

22	Little Charlie m 33 F m Head yes no
23	Chi-ki-kee f 48 F m wife yes no
24	Suc-leet-kee m 18 F s stp-son yes no

| 25 | Mary f 33 F w Head yes no |

26	Willie m 53 F w Head yes no
27	Suc-a-ti-yee f 26 F s dau yes no
28	John m 24 F s son yes no
29	Ruby f 22 F s dau yes no
30	La-ko-kee m 18 F s son yes no

1

Florida Seminoles Indian Census (As of April 1, 1930)

KEY: Census Number Name Sex Age at Last Birthday Tribe (Seminole, unless otherwise stated) Degree of Blood Marital Status Relationship to Head of Family At Jurisdiction where enrolled [Yes or No] (If no, Where) Ward [Yes or No] Allotment, Annuity, and Identification Numbers (if given).

31 Unknown f 13 F s dau yes no

32 Willie m 41 F m Head yes no
33 Unknown f 36 F m wife yes no
34 Unknown m 16 F s son yes no
35 Unknown m 12 F s son yes no

36 Yarber m 23 F m Head yes no
37 Unknown f 19 F m wife yes no
38 Unknown m 2 F s son yes no

BILLY

39 Grover m 34 F m Head yes no
40 Unknown f 24 F m wife yes no
41 Unknown m 13 F s son yes no
42 Unknown f 11 F s dau yes no

43 Ingram m 35 F m Head yes no
44 Tak-ho-kee f 34 F m wife yes no
45 Unknown f 20 F s dau yes no
46 Unknown f 18 F s dau yes no
47 Unknown m 16 F s son yes no
48 Unknown m 13 F s son yes no
49 Unknown m 9 F s son yes no
50 Unknown f 4 F s dau yes no

51 John m 85 F m Head yes no
52 Unknown f   F m wife yes no
53 Effie f 10 F s dau yes no
54 Unknown f 3 F s dau yes no

55 John m 35 F m Head yes no
56 Unknown f 33 F m wife yes no
57 Unknown m 15 F s son yes no
58 Unknown m 13 F s son yes no
59 Unknown f 11 F s dau yes no
60 Unknown m 8 F s son yes no
61 Unknown f 2 F s dau yes no

2

Florida Seminoles Indian Census (As of April 1, 1930)

KEY: Census Number Name Sex Age at Last Birthday Tribe (Seminole, unless otherwise stated) Degree of Blood Marital Status Relationship to Head of Family At Jurisdiction where enrolled [Yes or No] (If no, Where) Ward [Yes or No] Allotment, Annuity, and Identification Numbers (if given).

62	Unknown m 12 F s son yes no
63	Unknown f 28 F s sis-in-law yes no

64	Jose m 44 F m Head yes no
65	Wat-see f 40 F m wife yes no
66	Sta-vee f 12 F s dau yes no
67	E-sa-wee f 7 F s dau yes no
68	Unknown f 4 F s dau yes no
69	Unknown m 3 F s son yes no

70 Miami m 80 F w Head yes no

71	Robert m 29 F m Head yes no
72	Belle f 24 F m wife yes no
73	Unknown m 2 F s son yes no

74 Wilson m 28 F s Head yes no

BOLEGS

75	Billy m 68 F w Head yes no
76	Tucker, Lewis m 54 F s bro yes no
77	Pearce, Lucy f 38 F w sis yes no
78	Pearce, Ada f 19 F s niece yes no
79	Pearce, Anna f 17 F s niece yes no

BOWERS

80	Joe m 50 F m Head yes no
81	Lena f 31 F m wife yes no
82	Andrew Jackson m 21 F s son yes no
83	Lydee f 18 F s dau yes no
84	Dick m 14 F s son yes no
85	Unknown m 12 F s son yes no
86	Unknown m 10 F s son yes no
87	Unknown m 8 F s son yes no
88	Unknown m 6 F s son yes no

3

KEY: Census Number Name Sex Age at Last Birthday Tribe (Seminole, unless otherwise stated) Degree of Blood Marital Status Relationship to Head of Family At Jurisdiction where enrolled [Yes or No] (If no, Where) Ward [Yes or No] Allotment, Annuity, and Identification Numbers (if given).

BUCK

89   John m 32 F s Head yes no

90   Lena f 18 F w Head yes no

BUSTER

91   Billie m 64 F m Head yes no
92   Nellie f 79 F m wife yes no
93   Ar-nah 61 F s stp-dau yes no
94   Yek-am-kah 32 F s dau yes no
95   No-ket-cher f 31 F s dau yes no

96   Charlie m 55 F m Head yes no
97   Po-lah-lee f 50 F m wife yes no
98   Addie f 31 F s dau yes no
99   Little m 27 F s son yes no
100   Unknown f 23 F s dau yes no

101   Johnny m 33 F s Head yes no

102   Johnny m 40 F m Head yes no
103   In-git-tah-yee f 42 F m wife yes no
104   So-wah-ho-yee f 12 F s dau yes no
105   Unknown m 3 F s son yes no
106   Unknown m 1 F s son yes no

CHARLIE

107   Chief m 23 F m Head yes no
108   Rosalie f 33 F m wife yes no

CLAY

109   Henry m 55 F m Head yes no
110   Ka-ki-kee f 40 F m wife yes no
111   Abraham Lincoln m 32 F s son yes no
112   Jack Johnson m 26 F s son yes no

Florida Seminoles Indian Census (As of April 1, 1930)

KEY: Census Number Name Sex Age at Last Birthday Tribe (Seminole, unless otherwise stated) Degree of Blood Marital Status Relationship to Head of Family At Jurisdiction where enrolled [Yes or No] (If no, Where) Ward [Yes or No] Allotment, Annuity, and Identification Numbers (if given).

113   To-li-kee   f   24   F   s   dau   yes   no
114   Ta-li-kee   f   18   F   s   dau   yes   no
115   Nac-ho-mee   f   10   F   s   dau   yes   no

CYPRESS

116   Charlie   m   55   F   m   Head   yes   no
117   Lee   f   46   F   m   wife   yes   no
118   Buster Brown   m   16   F   s   son   yes   no
119   Unknown   f   14   F   s   dau   yes   no
120   Unknown   f   11   F   s   dau   yes   no
121   Unknown   f   2   F   s   dau   yes   no
122   Unknown   f   1   F   s   dau   yes   no
123   Futch   m   60   F   m   Head   yes   no
124   Unknown   f   43   F   m   wife   yes   no
125   Henry   m   25   F   s   son   yes   no
126   Harry   m   23   F   s   son   yes   no
127   Unknown   f   18   F   s   dau   yes   no

128   Johnny   m   28   F   m   Head   yes   no
129   My he-chee   f   26   F   m   wife   yes   no
130   Unknown   m   2   F   s   son   yes   no

131   Whitney   m   50   F   m   Head   yes   no
132   Sally   f   38   F   m   wife   yes   no
133   Suc-la-to-kee   f   16   F   s   dau   yes   no
134   See-ho-kee   f   14   F   s   dau   yes   no
135   Look-eet-see   m   11   F   s   son   yes   no
136   Che-na-see   f   9   F   s   dau   yes   no
137   Unknown   m   7   F   s   son   yes   no
138   Fewell, Billy   m   83   F   w   father-in-law   yes   no

139   Wilson   m   42   F   m   Head   yes   no
140   Ruby   f   32   F   m   wife   yes   no
141   Unknown   f   14   F   s   dau   yes   no
142   Unknown   f   13   F   s   dau   yes   no
143   Unknown   f   12   F   s   dau   yes   no
144   Unknown   m   7   F   s   son   yes   no

Florida Seminoles Indian Census (As of April 1, 1930)

KEY: Census Number Name Sex Age at Last Birthday Tribe (Seminole, unless otherwise stated) Degree of Blood Marital Status Relationship to Head of Family At Jurisdiction where enrolled [Yes or No] (If no, Where) Ward [Yes or No] Allotment, Annuity, and Identification Numbers (if given).

DIXIE

145	Charlie	m	58	¼	m	Head	yes	no
146	Jim-sling	f	53	F	m	wife	yes	no
147	Walter	m	26	¼	s	son	yes	no
148	Edwin	m	23	¼	s	son	yes	no
149	Susie	f	20	¼	s	dau	yes	no
150	Samson	m	8	¼	s	son	yes	no

DOCTOR

151	Cologne	m	34	F	m	Head	yes	no
152	Unknown	f	29	F	m	wife	yes	no
153	Unknown	m	14	F	s	son	yes	no
154	Unknown	m	10	F	s	son	yes	no
155	Unknown	m	7	F	s	son	yes	no
156	Unknown	f	6/12	F	s	dau	yes	no

157	Grover	m	40	F	m	Head	yes	no
158	Nac-o-tee	f	31	F	m	wife	yes	no
159	Unknown	m	8	F	s	son	yes	no
160	Unknown	f	7	F	s	dau	yes	no
161	Unknown	m	6/12	F	s	son	yes	no

162	Hal	m	35	F	m	Head	yes	no
163	Annie	f	35	F	m	wife	yes	no
164	Lat-I-kee	m	12	F	s	son	yes	no
165	Unknown	m	10	F	s	son	yes	no
166	Unknown	f	8	F	s	dau	yes	no
167	Co-sop-pee-chee	m	6	F	s	son	yes	no
168	She-cho-tee	m	4	F	s	son	yes	no

169	John	m	69	F	m	Head	yes	no
170	Unknown	f	49	F	m	wife	yes	no
171	Unknown	f	15	F	s	dau	yes	no
172	Unknown	f	13	F	s	dau	yes	no
173	Unknown	m	11	F	s	son	yes	no
174	Unknown	m	9	F	s	son	yes	no
175	Unknown	f	7	F	s	dau	yes	no

Florida Seminoles Indian Census (As of April 1, 1930)

KEY: Census Number Name Sex Age at Last Birthday Tribe (Seminole, unless otherwise stated) Degree of Blood Marital Status Relationship to Head of Family At Jurisdiction where enrolled [Yes or No] (If no, Where) Ward [Yes or No] Allotment, Annuity, and Identification Numbers (if given).

176 Little m 62 F m Head yes no
177 Mamie f 34 F m wife yes no
178 Tommie m 10 F s son yes no
179 Unknown f 8 F s dau yes no
180 Unknown f 6 F s dau yes no
181 Dorsie f 4 F s dau yes no

182 Wilson m 30 F m Head yes no
183 Unknown f 33 F m wife yes no

DRUITT

184 Jimmy m 30 F m Head yes no
185 Unknown f 18 F m wife yes no
186 **Motloe, Billy** m 75 F w father-in-law yes no

FEWELL

187 Charlie m 54 F m Head yes no
188 Lic-chee f 41 F m wife yes no
189 Le-to-kee f 24 F s dau yes no
190 John Philip m 24 F s stp-son yes no
191 Romeo m 22 F s stp-son yes no
192 Ko-hi-lee m 19 F s son yes no
193 Suc-tee m 17 F s son yes no
194 We-to-yee f 15 F s dau yes no
195 Git-ma-tee f 11 F s dau yes no

196 Johnny m 30 F m Head yes no
197 Eula f 26 F m wife yes no
198 Juanita f 5 F s dau yes no

FRANK

199 Miami m 50 F s Head yes no

FRAZIER

200 Bird m 25 F m Head yes no

7

Florida Seminoles Indian Census (As of April 1, 1930)

KEY: Census Number Name Sex Age at Last Birthday Tribe (Seminole, unless otherwise stated) Degree of Blood Marital Status Relationship to Head of Family At Jurisdiction where enrolled [Yes or No] (If no, Where) Ward [Yes or No] Allotment, Annuity, and Identification Numbers (if given).

201	Mon-o-la-kee f 21 F m wife yes no
202	Unknown m 3 F s son yes no
203	Unknown m 6/12 F s son yes no

GOPHER

204	Coffee m 45 F m Head yes no
205	Lucy f 47 F m wife yes no
206	Sar-a-chee m 25 F s son yes no
207	Som-fun-chee m 23 F s son yes no
208	Willie m 21 F s son yes no
209	San-to-sah-yee f 19 F s dau yes no
210	Ho-po-yo-yee f 17 F s dau yes no
211	Carlisle Jim m 14 F s son yes no
212	Unknown 12 f s grnd-dau yes no

213	Jim m 60 F w Head yes no
214	Ada f 32 F s dau yes no
215	**Tiger, Mary** f 71 F w sister yes no
216	**Tiger, Ada** f 31 F s niece yes no
217	**Tiger, Betty Mae** f 9 ¼ s grnd-niece yes no
218	**Tiger, Howard** m 5 ¼ grnd-nephew yes no

HALLS

| 219 | Oscar m 69 F s Head yes no |

HENRY

220	Jim m 40 F m Head yes no
221	Tim-a-kee f 30 F m wife yes no
222	Unknown f 9 F s dau yes no
223	Unknown m 7 F s son yes no

HUFF

224	Sam m 47 F w Head yes no
225	Poca-hontas f 21 F s dau yes no
226	Frank m 17 F s son yes no

8

KEY: Census Number Name Sex Age at Last Birthday Tribe (Seminole, unless otherwise stated) Degree of Blood Marital Status Relationship to Head of Family At Jurisdiction where enrolled [Yes or No] (If no, Where) Ward [Yes or No] Allotment, Annuity, and Identification Numbers (if given).

227   Alice f 15 F s dau yes no
228   George m 2 F s grnd-son yes no

JIM

229   Billie m 40 F m Head yes no
230   Unknown f 37 F m wife yes no
231   Unknown f 10 F s dau yes no
232   Unknown f 7 F s dau yes no
233   Unknown f 5 F s dau yes no

234   Frank m 29 F s Head yes no

235   Lazy m 34 F m Head yes no
236   Mon-ta-kee f 28 F m wife yes no
237   Unknown f 12 F s dau yes no
238   Unknown f 11 F s dau yes no
239   Ah-po-kee f 17 F s niece yes no

240   Miami m 88 F w Head yes no
241   Jose m 35 F s son yes no

242   Webb m 33 F m Head yes no
243   Unknown f 28 F m wife yes no
244   Unknown m 11 F s son yes no
245   Unknown m 9 F s son yes no
246   Unknown f 7 F s dau yes no
247   Unknown f 4 F s dau yes no

248   Willie m 32 F m Head yes no
249   Unknown f 19 F m wife yes no

JIMMIE

250   Little m 30 F m Head yes no
251   Unknown f 28 F m wife yes no
252   Unknown m 12 F s dau yes no
253   Unknown m 10 F s son yes no

Florida Seminoles Indian Census (As of April 1, 1930)

KEY: Census Number Name Sex Age at Last Birthday Tribe (Seminole, unless otherwise stated) Degree of Blood Marital Status Relationship to Head of Family At Jurisdiction where enrolled [Yes or No] (If no, Where) Ward [Yes or No] Allotment, Annuity, and Identification Numbers (if given).

JOHNNY

254	Kir-kee	m	35	F	s	Head	yes	no
255	Sar-pi-kul-ker	f	39	F	s	sister	yes	no
256	Ma-har	f	37	F	s	sister	yes	no

JOHNS

257	Ernie	f	42	F	s	Head	yes	no
258	Willie	m	59	F	m	Head	yes	no
259	Anne	f	64	F	m	wife	yes	no
260	Fik-heth-lee	f	32	F	s	dau	yes	no
261	Oscar	m	28	F	s	son	yes	no
262	Unknown	f	26	F	s	dau	yes	no
263	Unknown	f	24	F	s	dau	yes	no
264	Mok-har-po-kee	f	22	F	s	dau	yes	no
265	Sac-che-wah	m	20	F	s	son	yes	no
266	Ka-see-ha-chee	f	18	F	s	dau	yes	no
267	Ar-nah	f	16	F	s	dau	yes	no
268	In-kar-pak-kee	m	14	F	s	son	yes	no
269	Lizzie	f	11	F	s	dau	yes	no
270	Unknown	f	9	F	s	dau	yes	no
271	Unknown	f	6/12	F	s	gr-dau	yes	no

JONES

272	Sam	m	36	F	m	Head	yes	no
273	Missie Stick	f	34	F	m	wife	yes	no
274	Free	f	16	F	s	dau	yes	no
275	Willie	m	13	F	s	son	yes	no
276	Unknown	m	10	F	s	son	yes	no
277	Unknown	f	8	F	s	dau	yes	no
278	Unknown	f	6	F	s	dau	yes	no
279	Unknown	f	4	F	s	dau	yes	no
280	Unknown	f	2	F	s	dau	yes	no
281	Unknown	m	1	F	s	son	yes	no
282	Sam	m	80	F	w	cousin	yes	no

Florida Seminoles Indian Census (As of April 1, 1930)

KEY: Census Number Name Sex Age at Last Birthday Tribe (Seminole, unless otherwise stated) Degree of Blood Marital Status Relationship to Head of Family At Jurisdiction where enrolled [Yes or No] (If no, Where) Ward [Yes or No] Allotment, Annuity, and Identification Numbers (if given).

JOSH

283   John m 21 ¼ s Head yes no

JUMPER

284   Mrs. Squirrel f 50 F w Head yes no
285   Stem-i-he-ooh f 30 F s dau yes no
286   Unknown m 27 F s son yes no

287   Charlie m 65 F m Head yes no
288   Wa-to-kee f 58 F m Head yes no
289   Boy m 28 F s stp-son yes no
290   Buffalo Bill m 25 F s stp-son yes no

291   Charlie f 48 F m Head yes no
292   Sally f 39 F m wife yes no
293   Charlie Knight m 21 F s son yes no
294   Unknown m 19 F s son yes no
295   Unknown f 16 F s dau yes no
296   Unknown m 14 F s son yes no
297   Ruby f 12 F s dau yes no
298   Unknown m 8 F s dau yes no

299   Cooter m 43 F m Head yes no

300   Unknown f 50 F m Head yes no
301   Unknown m 38 F s stp-son yes no
302   Miami Charlie m 28 F s son yes no
303   Unknown f 23 F s dau yes no
304   Unknown f 21 F s dau yes no

305   John Joy m 25 F s Head yes no
306   Figi f 55 F w mother yes no

307   Josie m 25 F m Head yes no
308   Katie f 24 F m wife yes no
309   Moses m 3 F s son yes no

11

Florida Seminoles Indian Census (As of April 1, 1930)

KEY: Census Number Name Sex Age at Last Birthday Tribe (Seminole, unless otherwise stated) Degree of Blood Marital Status Relationship to Head of Family At Jurisdiction where enrolled [Yes or No] (If no, Where) Ward [Yes or No] Allotment, Annuity, and Identification Numbers (if given).

310   Willie m 60 F s Head yes no

McKINLEY

311   William m 35 F m Head yes no
312   To-wee f 28 F m wife yes no
313   Homer m 13 F s son yes no
314   Mitty f 11 F s dau yes no
315   Dixie m 9 F s son yes no
316   Douglas m 6 F s son yes no
317   Unknown m 3 F s son yes no

MICCO

318   Charlie m 38 F m Head yes no
319   Was-wah-kee f 30 F m wife yes no
320   Sake-lat-kee f 15 F s dau yes no
321   Unknown f 13 F s dau yes no
322   Unknown f 11 F s dau yes no
323   Unknown f 9 F s dau yes no
324   To-tho-po-ho-chee m 6 F s son yes no
325   Little Jack m 1 F s son yes no

326   Oscar m 33 F m Head yes no
327   To-chee f 30 F m wife yes no
328   Unknown f 12 F s dau yes no
329   Unknown f 10 F s dau yes no
330   Unknown f 8 F s dau yes no
331   Unknown f 6 F s dau yes no
332   Unknown m 4 F s son yes no

MORGAN

333   Eli m 36 F s Head yes no
334   Unknown f 70 F w mother yes no
335   Jake m 34 F s brother yes no
336   Ma-ma f 24 F s sister yes no
337   **Hilliard, Sheela Johns** f 32 F w sister-in-law yes no

Florida Seminoles Indian Census (As of April 1, 1930)

KEY: Census Number Name Sex Age at Last Birthday Tribe (Seminole, unless otherwise stated) Degree of Blood Marital Status Relationship to Head of Family At Jurisdiction where enrolled [Yes or No] (If no, Where) Ward [Yes or No] Allotment, Annuity, and Identification Numbers (if given).

MOTLOE

338   Jack m 36 F m Head yes no
339   Belle f 34 F m wife yes no
340   Ollie f 4 F s stp-dau yes no

341   John m 30 F s Head yes no
342   Jennie Jumper f 45 F w cousin yes no

OSCEOLA

343   Billie m 38 F m Head yes no
344   Ruby f 34 F m wife yes no
345   Tak-hat-a-see f 19 F s dau yes no
346   Unknown f 16 F s dau yes no
347   Che-ho-kee m 14 F s son yes no
348   Unknown f 12 F s dau yes no
349   Unknown m 10 F s son yes no
350   Unknown m 8 F s son yes no
351   Jimmie m 6 F s son yes no

352   Billy m 40 F m Head yes no
353   Sally f 37 F m wife yes no
354   Unknown f 12 F s dau yes no
355   Unknown f 10 F s dau yes no
356   Unknown m 8 F s son yes no

357   Charlie m 23 F m Head yes no
358   Tommie Hand f 31 F m wife yes no
359   Unknown f 5 F s stp-dau yes no
360   Unknown m 3 F s stp-son yes no
361   Unknown f 2 F s stp-dau yes no

362   Cory m 25 F m Head yes no
363   Juanita f 21 F m wife yes no
364   Unknown f 1 F s dau yes no

365   George m 50 F m Head yes no
366   Non-for-me f 39 F m wife yes no

Florida Seminoles Indian Census (As of April 1, 1930)

KEY: Census Number Name Sex Age at Last Birthday Tribe (Seminole, unless otherwise stated) Degree of Blood Marital Status Relationship to Head of Family At Jurisdiction where enrolled [Yes or No] (If no, Where) Ward [Yes or No] Allotment, Annuity, and Identification Numbers (if given).

367   Par-tah-see f 18 F s dau yes no
368   Ba-sof-tee m 16 F s son yes no
369   Unknown f 11 F s dau yes no

370   Jim-joy m 36 F m Head yes no
371   Unknown f 33 F m wife yes no
372   Unknown f 17 F s dau yes no
373   Unknown f 15 F s dau yes no
374   Unknown m 11 F s son yes no

375   Jimmie m 82 F w Head yes no
376   Sar-ho-kee-see m 17 F s son yes no
378   Lizzie f 15 F s dau yes no
379   Stuman m 13 F s son yes no
380   Richard m 11 F s son yes no

381   John m 60 F m Head yes no
382   Chaw-see f 50 F m wife yes no
383   Robert m 19 F s son yes no
384   Te-ki-kee f 15 F s dau yes no
385   Loc-kee m 13 F s son yes no
386   Wah-tee f 11 F s dau yes no
387   Unknown f 6 F s dau yes no

388   John m 48 F m Head yes no
389   Unknown f 48 F m wife yes no
390   Unknown f 25 F s dau yes no
391   Unknown f 20 F s dau yes no
392   Pal-i-kee m 13 F s son yes no

393   Wit-kee f 38 F w Head yes no
394   Unknown f 21 F s dau yes no

PARKER

395   Argyl ,m 30 F s Head yes no
396   Amelia f 34 F s sister yes no
397   Dan m 36 F w Head yes no

14

Florida Seminoles Indian Census (As of April 1, 1930)

KEY: Census Number Name Sex Age at Last Birthday Tribe (Seminole, unless otherwise stated) Degree of Blood Marital Status Relationship to Head of Family At Jurisdiction where enrolled [Yes or No] (If no, Where) Ward [Yes or No] Allotment, Annuity, and Identification Numbers (if given).

PEACOCK

398   Charlie m 35 F s Head yes no

PLATT

399   Josh m 26 ¼ s Head yes no
400   Fi-kee f 69 ¼ w mother yes no

PRETTY

401   Old f 62 F w Head yes no

ROBERTS

402   Kar-nac-tee f 22 F s Head yes no
403   To-pi-kee f 20 F s sister yes no
404   Nat-cho-kee m 14 F s brother yes no
405   Lak-kee m 11 F s brother yes no

SMITH

406   Billie m 80 F m Head yes no
407   Mut-to-lo-kee f 75 F m wife yes no
408   Dolly f 47 F s dau yes no
409   Dick m 49 F m Head yes no
410   Hon-kee f 45 F m wife yes no
411   Lobie f 14 F s dau yes no
412   Wa-chee m 12 F s son yes no

413   Morgan m 30 F m Head yes no
414   Unknown f 25 F m wife yes no
415   Unknown f ?/12 F s dau yes no

416   Tom m 41 F m Head yes no
417   Stella f 30 F m wife yes no
418   Unknown f 3 F s dau yes no
419   Unknown f 1 F s dau yes no
420   Cully f 32 F s sister yes no

Florida Seminoles Indian Census (As of April 1, 1930)

KEY: Census Number Name Sex Age at Last Birthday Tribe (Seminole, unless otherwise stated) Degree of Blood Marital Status Relationship to Head of Family At Jurisdiction where enrolled [Yes or No] (If no, Where) Ward [Yes or No] Allotment, Annuity, and Identification Numbers (if given).

SNOW

421 Samson m 34 F m Head yes no
422 Co-pic-cha-ho-lee f 29 F m wife yes no
423 Chat-lah-nok-kee f 1 F s dau yes no

STEWART

424 Billie m 55 F m Head yes no
425 Susie f 51 f m wife yes no
426 Fannie f 28 F s dau yes no
427 Am-a-chee f 90 F w mother yes no
428 **Charlie, Big** m 47 F s brother-in-law yes no
429 **Snow, Charlie** m 34 F s nephew yes no
430 **Wells, Ben** m 21 F s nephew yes no

TIGER

431 Brown m 40 F w Head yes no
432 Unknown f 12 F s stp-dau yes no
433 Unknown m 9 F s stp-son yes no

434 Charlie m 48 F w Head yes no
435 Unknown m 7 F s son yes no

436 Cuffney m 52 F m Head yes no
437 Unknown f 12(?) F m wife yes no
438 Unknown f 20 F s dau yes no

439 Doctor m 51 F w Head yes no

440 Emma f 40 F w Head yes no
441 Unknown f 20 F s dau yes no
442 Unknown m 18 F s son yes no

443 Frank m 39 F w Head yes no
444 John Frank m 19 F s son yes no
445 Unknown f 17 F s dau yes no
446 Unknown f 15 F s dau yes no

16

Florida Seminoles Indian Census (As of April 1, 1930)

KEY: Census Number Name Sex Age at Last Birthday Tribe (Seminole, unless otherwise stated) Degree of Blood Marital Status Relationship to Head of Family At Jurisdiction where enrolled [Yes or No] (If no, Where) Ward [Yes or No] Allotment, Annuity, and Identification Numbers (if given).

447 Unknown f 13 F s dau yes no
448 Unknown m 11 F s son yes no
449 Jim m 48 F m Head yes no
450 Unknown f 58 F m wife yes no
451 Little m 27 F s son yes no
452 Unknown f 26 F s dau yes no
453 Unknown m 22 F s son yes no
454 Unknown m 18 F s son yes no

455 Miami John m 53 F m Head yes no
456 Unknown f 44 F m wife yes no
457 Unknown m 22 F s son yes no
458 Unknown m 18 F s son yes no
459 Unknown m 16 F s son yes no
460 Unknown f 14 F s dau yes no
461 Willie m 60 F w brother-in-law yes no
462 **Billie, Homespun** m 39 F s brother-in-law yes no

463 Nac-o-tee f 37 F w Head yes no
464 Unknown m 20 F s son yes no
465 Unknown f 16 F s dau yes no
466 Unknown m 14 F s son yes no
467 Unknown f 12 F s dau yes no

468 Na-ha m 44 F m Head yes no

469 Lucy f 52 F m Head yes no

470 Santee m 28 F s Head yes no

471 Tiger m 35 F m Head yes no
472 Ruby f 32 F m wife yes no
473 Tiger Boy m 15 F s son yes no
474 Mar-stook-kee f 13 F s dau yes no
475 Frank m 11 F s son yes no
476 Josie m 9 F s son yes no
477 Cypress m 7 F s son yes no
478 Harjo m 5 F s son yes no
479 Unknown f 3 F s dau yes no

Florida Seminoles Indian Census (As of April 1, 1930)

KEY: Census Number Name Sex Age at Last Birthday Tribe (Seminole, unless otherwise stated) Degree of Blood Marital Status Relationship to Head of Family At Jurisdiction where enrolled [Yes or No] (If no, Where) Ward [Yes or No] Allotment, Annuity, and Identification Numbers (if given).

TIGERTAIL

480	Charlie m 60 F w Head yes no
481	Cat-ath-lee m 14 F s son yes no
482	Wilson m 18 F m Head yes no
483	Na-ha-we f 17 F m wife yes no
484	Doc Wilson m 26 F s half-bro yes no
485	Unknown f 24 F s half-sis yes no
486	Unknown m 20 F s brother yes no
487	Unknown f 16 F s sister yes no
488	Unknown f 14 F s sister yes no
489	Unknown f 12 F s sister yes no
490	Unknown f 9 F s sister yes no

TOMMIE

491	Anna f 74 F w Head yes no
492	Annie May f 37 F s dau yes no
493	Brownie m 31 f s son yes no

494	Ben Frank m 47 F m Head yes no
495	Tudie f 35 F m wife yes no
496	Mary f 8 F s dau yes no
497	**Tiger, Missie** f 42 F s sister-in-law yes no
498	**Parker, Mary** f 8 F s niece yes no
499	**Parker, Agnes** f 6 F s niece yes no

| 500 | Charlie m 50 F w Head yes no |
| 501 | Unknown f 13 F s dau yes no |

| 502 | Charlie m 57 F s Head yes no |

| 503 | Charlie m 56 F m Head yes no |
| 504 | Cho-bee f 52 F m wife yes no |

505	Frank m 34 F m Head yes no
506	Ho-mi-pee f 24 F m wife yes no
507	Willie Micco m 3 F s son yes no
508	Es-tah-kah-yee m 4/12 F s son yes no

18

Florida Seminoles Indian Census (As of April 1, 1930)

KEY: Census Number Name Sex Age at Last Birthday Tribe (Seminole, unless otherwise stated) Degree of Blood Marital Status Relationship to Head of Family At Jurisdiction where enrolled [Yes or No] (If no, Where) Ward [Yes or No] Allotment, Annuity, and Identification Numbers (if given).

509   Jack m 32 F m Head yes no
510   Unknown f 25 F m wife yes no
511   Unknown m 10 F s son yes no
512   Unknown m 8 F s son yes no
513   Unknown m 6 F s son yes no
514   Unknown f 5 F s dau yes no
515   Unknown m 3 F s son yes no
516   Herbert Hoover m 1 F s son yes no
517   **Chippo, Emma** f 69 F 2 mother-in-law yes no

518   Jim m 34 F n Head yes no
519   Lo-bee f 26 F m wife yes no
520   Unknown m 3 F s son yes no

521   Jimmie m 34 F m Head yes no
522   Unknown f 35 F m wife yes no
523   Unknown m 4 F s son yes no

524   Lady f 26 F s Head yes no
525   Morgan Baby f 5 F s dau yes no

526   Sam m 25 F m Head yes no
527   Melid f 16 F m wife yes no

528   Tony m 30 F Head no Wetumka City, OK no

529   Small-pox m 43 F m Head yes no
530   Mary f 35 F m wife yes no

TONY

531   Young m 48 F m Head yes no
532   Unknown f 43 F m wife yes no
533   Sim-pa-ha-he f 17 F s dau yes no
534   Cla-sa-ho-yee f 11 F s dau yes no
535   Jimmie Billie m 30 F s nephew yes no
536   Unknown m 28 F s nephew yes no
537   Unknown f 25 F s niece yes no
538   Jimmie Doctor m 23 F s nephew yes no

KEY: Census Number Name Sex Age at Last Birthday Tribe (Seminole, unless otherwise stated) Degree of Blood Marital Status Relationship to Head of Family At Jurisdiction where enrolled [Yes or No] (If no, Where) Ward [Yes or No] Allotment, Annuity, and Identification Numbers (if given).

TUCKER

539	Billy m 49 F m Head yes no
540	Susie f 28 F m wife yes no
541	Chaw-huck-kee f 69 F w mother yes no
542	Ho-po-thut-kee f 52 F s sister yes no
543	Mait-kah f 50 F s sister yes no
544	Sar-thler-nah-kee f 26 F s sister yes no
545	Frank m 24 F s brother yes no
546	Nok-me-lee-kee m 24 F s nephew yes no
547	Te-heth-lee-kee f 22 F s niece yes no

548	Oscar m 34 F m Head yes no
549	Cotner f 31 F m wife yes no
550	Cus-sum-lak-chee f 15 F s dau yes no
551	Unknown m 12 F s son yes no
552	Unknown m 9 F s son yes no
553	Unknown m 6 F s son yes no

WALKER

554	Henry m 62 F m Head yes no
555	Unknown f 50 F m wife yes no
556	Unknown f 26 F s dau yes no

| 557 | Wat-cha-kee m 28 F Head yes no |

WILLIE

558	Frank m 45 F m Head yes no
559	Ruby f 39 F m wife yes no
560	O-mas-kee m 15 F s son yes no
561	Yo-pote-ama f 11 F s dau yes no
562	Little f 1 F s dau yes no

563	Jesse m 30 F m Head yes no
564	Unknown f 27 F m wife yes no
565	Unknown f 10 F s dau yes no
566	Unknown f 9 F s dau yes no

Florida Seminoles Indian Census (As of April 1, 1930)

KEY: Census Number Name Sex Age at Last Birthday Tribe (Seminole, unless otherwise stated) Degree of Blood Marital Status Relationship to Head of Family At Jurisdiction where enrolled [Yes or No] (If no, Where) Ward [Yes or No] Allotment, Annuity, and Identification Numbers (if given).

567   Johnny m 60 F w Head yes no

568   Sam m 38 F m Head yes no
569   Unknown f 30 F m wife yes no
570   Henry m 11 F s son yes no
571   Walter Roy m 8 F s son yes no
572   John m 7 F s son yes no
573   Mary f 5 F s dau yes no
574   Unknown m 3 F s son yes no
575   **Charlie, Corinne** f 24 F w sister-in-law yes no
576   **Charlie, Pauline** f 4 F s niece yes no

WILSON

577   Ben m 26 F s Head yes no
578   Yu-pak-lat-kah m 53 F w father yes no

KEY: Census Number Name Sex Age at Last Birthday Tribe (Seminole, unless otherwise stated)
Degree of Blood Marital Status Relationship to Head of Family At Jurisdiction where enrolled
[Yes or No] (If no, Where) Ward [Yes or No] Allotment, Annuity, and Identification Numbers (if
given).

BILLIE

1	Sac-a-to-yee	f	31	F	w	Head	yes	no
2	Unknown	m	12	F	s	son	yes	no
3	Unknown	m	10	F	s	son	yes	no
4	Unknown	f	8	F	s	dau	yes	no
5	Unknown	m	6	F	s	son	yes	no
6	Unknown	f	4	F	s	dau	yes	no
7	Unknown	f	5/12	F	s	dau	yes	no
8	Rosalie	f	17	F	s	sis	yes	no
9	Charley	m	51	F	m	Head	yes	no
10	Mona	f	47	F	m	wife	yes	no
11	Chestnut	m	25	F	s	son	yes	no
12	Ruby	f	23	F	s	dau	yes	no
13	Maggie	f	19	F	s	dau	yes	no
14	Cowboy	m	21	F	m	Head	yes	no
15	Annie	f	15	F	m	wife	yes	no
16	Girtman	m	35	F	w	Head	yes	no
17	To-hi-kee	m	13	F	s	son	yes	no
18	Kunzie	m	35	F	m	Head	yes	no
19	Addie	f	35	F	m	wife	yes	no
20	Unknown	m	9	F	s	son	yes	no
21	Unknown	f	1	F	s	dau	yes	no
22	Little Charlie	m	34	F	m	Head	yes	no
23	Chi-ki-kee	f	49	F	m	wife	yes	no
24	Suc-leet-kee	m	19	F	s	son	yes	no
25	Mary	f	34	F	w	Head	yes	no
26	Willie	m	54	F	w	Head	yes	no
27	John	m	25	F	s	son	yes	no
28	Ruby	f	14	F	s	dau	yes	no
29	Unknown	f	9	F	s	dau	yes	no

KEY: Census Number Name Sex Age at Last Birthday Tribe (Seminole, unless otherwise stated) Degree of Blood Marital Status Relationship to Head of Family At Jurisdiction where enrolled [Yes or No] (If no, Where) Ward [Yes or No] Allotment, Annuity, and Identification Numbers (if given).

```
30  Willie m 42 F m Head yes no
31  Unknown f 37 F m wife yes no
32  Unknown m 17 F s son yes no
33  Unknown m 13 F s son yes no
34  Yarber m 24 F m Head yes no
35  Unknown f 19 F m wife yes no
36  Unknown m 3 F s son yes no
```

BILLY

```
37  Grover m 35 F m Head yes no
38  Unknown f 25 F m wife yes no
39  Unknown m 14 F s son yes no
40  Unknown f 12 F s dau yes no

41  Ingram 36 F m Head yes no
42  Tak-ho-kee f 35 F m wife yes no
43  Unknown f 21 F s dau yes no
44  Unknown f 19 F s dau yes no
45  Unknown m 17 F s son yes no
46  Unknown m 14 F s son yes no
47  Unknown m 10 F s son yes no
48  Unknown f 5 F s dau yes no

49  John m 86 F m Head yes no
50  Mah-won-a-ha-yee f 18 F n wife yes no
51  Effie f 6 F s dau yes no
52  Unknown f 4 F s dau yes no

53  John m 36 F m Head yes no
54  Unknown f 34 F m wife yes no
55  Unknown m 9 F s son yes no
56  Unknown f 3 F s dau yes no
57  Unknown f 29 F s sis-in-law yes no

58  Jose m 45 F m Head yes no
59  Wat-see f 41 F m wife yes no
60  Sta-vee f 13 F s dau yes no
```

Florida Seminoles Indian Census (As of April 1, 1931)

KEY: Census Number Name Sex Age at Last Birthday Tribe (Seminole, unless otherwise stated) Degree of Blood Marital Status Relationship to Head of Family At Jurisdiction where enrolled [Yes or No] (If no, Where) Ward [Yes or No] Allotment, Annuity, and Identification Numbers (if given).

61 E-sa-wee f 8 F s dau yes no
62 Unknown f 5 F s dau yes no
63 Unknown m 4 F s son yes no

64 Robert m 30 F m Head yes no
65 Unknown f 31 F m wife yes no
66 Wilson m 19 F s Head yes no

BOLEGS

67 Billy m 69 1/4 w Head yes no
68 **Tucker, Lewis** m 55 1/4 F[sic] bro yes no
69 **Pearce, Lucy** f 39 F w sis yes no
70 **Pearce, Ada** f 20 F s niece yes no
71 **Pearce, Anna** f 18 F s niece yes no
72 **Osceola, Richard** m 26 F s nephew yes no

BOWERS

73 Joe m 51 F m Head yes no
74 Lena f 32 F m wife yes no
75 Andres Jackson m 2 F w son yes no
76 Lydee f 19 f s dau yes no
77 Dick m 15 F s son yes no
78 Unknown m 13 F s son yes no
79 Unknown m 1 F s son yes no
80 Unknown m 9 F s son yes no
81 Unknown m 7 F s son yes no

82 Lillie f 35 F w Head yes no
83 **Buster, Tom** m 12 F s son yes no
84 **Buster, Bessie** f 6 F s dau yes no
85 **Willie, Ruby** f 40 F w sis yes no
86 **Willie, Little** f 2 F s niece yes no

BUCK

87 John m 33 F m Head yes no

Florida Seminoles Indian Census (As of April 1, 1931)

KEY: Census Number Name Sex Age at Last Birthday Tribe (Seminole, unless otherwise stated) Degree of Blood Marital Status Relationship to Head of Family At Jurisdiction where enrolled [Yes or No] (If no, Where) Ward [Yes or No] Allotment, Annuity, and Identification Numbers (if given).

88   Unknown f 14 F m wife yes no
89   Lena f 19 F w Alone yes no

BUSTER

90   Billie m 65 F m Head yes no
91   Nellie f 80 F m wife yes no
92   Ar-nah f 62 F s stp-dau yes no
93   Yek-am-kah f 33 F s dau yes no
94   No-ket-cher f 33 F s dau yes no

95   Charlie m 56 F m Head yes no
96   Po-lah-lee f 51 F m wife yes no
97   Addie f 32 F s dau yes no
98   Little f 28 F s dau yes no
99   Unknown f 24 F s dau yes no

100   Johnny m 34 F s Head yes no

101   Johnny m 41 F m Head yes no
102   In-git-tah-yee f 43 F m wife yes no
103   So-wah-ho-yee f 13 F s dau yes no
104   Unknown m 4 F s son yes no
105   Unknown m 2 F s son yes no

CHARLIE

106   Chief m 24 F m Head yes no
107   Rosalie f 34 F m wife *(yes/no omitted)*

108   Frank m 20 F m Head yes no
109   Carrie f 15 F m wife yes no

CLAY

110   Henry m 56 F m Head yes no
111   Ka-ki-kee f 41 F m wife yes no
112   Abraham Lincoln m 33 F s son yes no

25

KEY: Census Number Name Sex Age at Last Birthday Tribe (Seminole, unless otherwise stated) Degree of Blood Marital Status Relationship to Head of Family At Jurisdiction where enrolled [Yes or No] (If no, Where) Ward [Yes or No] Allotment, Annuity, and Identification Numbers (if given).

113	Jack Johnson	m	27	F	s	son	yes	no	
114	To-li-kee	f	25	F	s	dau	yes	no	
115	Ta-la-kee	f	19	F	s	dau	yes	no	
116	Nac-ho-mee	f	11	F	s	dau	yes	no	

CYPRESS

117	Charlie	m	56	F	m	Head	yes	no	
118	Lee	f	47	F	m	wife	yes	no	
119	Henry	m	17	F	s	son	yes	no	
120	Unknown	f	12	F	s	dau	yes	no	
121	Tomafino	f	5	F	s	dau	yes	no	
122	Stanley Hanson	m	3	F	s	son	yes	no	
123	Futch	m	61	F	m	Head	yes	no	
124	Unknown	f	44	F	m	wife	yes	no	
125	Henry	m	26	F	s	son	yes	no	
126	Harry	m	24	F	s	son	yes	no	
127	Unknown	f	19	F	s	dau	yes	no	
128	Johnny	m	29	F	m	Head	yes	no	
129	My-ho-chee	f	27	F	m	wife	yes	no	
130	Unknown	m	9	F	s	son	yes	no	
131	Unknown	m	3	F	s	son	yes	no	
132	Whitney	m	51	F	m	Head	yes	no	
133	Sally	f	39	F	m	wife	yes	no	
134	Suc-la-to-kee	f	17	F	s	dau	yes	no	
135	See-ho-kee	f	15	F	s	dau	yes	no	
136	Look-eet-see	m	12	F	s	son	yes	no	
137	Che-na-see	f	10	F	s	dau	yes	no	
138	Unknown	m	8	F	s	son	yes	no	
139	**Fewell, Billy**	m	92	F	w	father-in-law	yes	no	
140	Wilson	m	43	F	m	Head	yes	no	
141	Ruby	f	33	F	m	wife	yes	no	
142	Unknown	f	15	F	s	dau	yes	no	
143	Unknown	f	14	F	s	dau	yes	no	
144	Unknown	f	13	F	s	dau	yes	no	

KEY: Census Number Name Sex Age at Last Birthday Tribe (Seminole, unless otherwise stated) Degree of Blood Marital Status Relationship to Head of Family At Jurisdiction where enrolled [Yes or No] (If no, Where) Ward [Yes or No] Allotment, Annuity, and Identification Numbers (if given).

145   Unknown m 8 F s son yes no

DIXIE

146   Charlie m 59 ¼ m Head yes no
147   Jim-sling f 54 F m wife yes no
148   Walter m 26 ¼ s son yes no
149   Edwin m 24 ¼ s son yes no
150   Susie f 21 ¼ s dau yes no
151   Samson m 9 ¼ s son yes no
152   **Billy, Mrs. Miami** f 96 F w mother-in-law yes no

DOCTOR

153   Cologne m 35 F m Head yes no
154   Unknown f 30 F m wife yes no
155   Unknown m 15 F s son yes no
156   Unknown m 11 F s son yes no
157   Unknown m 8 F s son yes no
158   Unknown f 1 F s dau yes no
159   Grover m 41 F m Head yes no
160   Nac-o-tee f 32 F m wife yes no
161   Unknown m 9 F s son yes no
162   Unknown f 8 F s dau yes no
163   Unknown m 1 F s son yes no

164   Hal m 36 F m Head yes no
165   Annie f 36 F m wife yes no
166   Lat-i-kee m 13 F s son yes no
167   Unknown m 11 F s son yes no
168   Unknown f 9 F s dau yes no
169   Co-sop-cho-tee m 7 F s son yes no
170   She-cho-pee m 5 F s son yes no

171   Unknown f 50 F w wife yes no
172   Unknown m 12 F s son yes no
173   Unknown m 10 F s son yes no
174   Unknown f 8 F s dau yes no

Florida Seminoles Indian Census (As of April 1, 1931)

KEY: Census Number Name Sex Age at Last Birthday Tribe (Seminole, unless otherwise stated) Degree of Blood Marital Status Relationship to Head of Family At Jurisdiction where enrolled [Yes or No] (If no, Where) Ward [Yes or No] Allotment, Annuity, and Identification Numbers (if given).

175   Little m 63 F m Head yes no
176   Mamie f 35 F m wife yes no
177   Unknown f 18 F s dau yes no
178   Unknown f 16 F s dau yes no
179   Tommie m 14 F s son yes no

180   Wilson m 31 F m Head yes no
181   Unknown f 32 F m wife yes no
182   Unknown f 5 F s dau yes no

DRUITT

183   Jimmy m 31 F m Head yes no
184   Unknown f 19 F m wife yes no
185   Unknown f 9 F s dau yes no
186   Unknown m 7 F s son yes no
187   Unknown m 3 F s son yes no
188   **Motloe, Billy** m 76 F w father-in-law yes no

FEWELL

189   Charlie m 5 F m Head yes no
190   Lic-chee f 42 F m wife yes no
191   John Philip m 25 F s stp-son yes no
192   Romeo m 23 F s stp-son yes no
193   Ko-hi-lee m 20 F s son yes no
194   Suc-tee m 18 F s son yes no
195   We-to-yee f 16 F s dau yes no
196   Git-ma-tee f 12 F s dau yes no

197   Johnny m 31 F m Head yes no
198   Eula f 27 F m wife yes no
199   Juanita f 6 F s dau yes no

FRANK

200   Miami m 51 F s Head yes no

Florida Seminoles Indian Census (As of April 1, 1931)

KEY: Census Number Name Sex Age at Last Birthday Tribe (Seminole, unless otherwise stated) Degree of Blood Marital Status Relationship to Head of Family At Jurisdiction where enrolled [Yes or No] (If no, Where) Ward [Yes or No] Allotment, Annuity, and Identification Numbers (if given).

FRAZIER

201	Bird m 26 F w Head yes no
202	Unknown m 4 F s son yes no
203	Unknown m 1 F s son yes no

GOPHER

201 Bird m 26 F w Head yes no
202 Unknown m 4 F s son yes no
203 Unknown m 1 F s son yes no

204 Jim m 61 F w Head yes no
205 Ada f 33 F s dau yes no
206 **Tiger, Mary** f 71 F w sis yes no
207 **Tiger, Ada** f 32 F s niece yes no
208 **Tiger, Betty Mae** f 10 ¼ s grt-niece yes no
209 [sic] Howard m 7 ¼ grt-nephew yes no

210 Lucy f 48 F w wife yes no
211 Sar-a-chee m 26 F s son yes no
212 Som-fun-chee m 24 F s son yes no
213 Willie m 22 F s son yes no
214 San-to-sah-yee f 20 F s dau yes no
215 Ho-po-yo-yee f 18 F s dau yes no
216 Carlisle Jim m 15 F s son yes no
217 Unknown f 1 F s grnd-dau yes no

HENRY

218 Jim m 41 F m Head yes no
219 Tim-a-kee f 31 F m wife yes no
220 Unknown f 10 F s dau yes no
221 Unknown m 8 F s son yes no

HUFF

222 Sam m 48 F w Head yes no
223 Poca-hontas f 22 F s dau yes no
224 Frank m 18 F s son yes no
225 George m 3 F s grnd-son yes no

29

Florida Seminoles Indian Census (As of April 1, 1931)

KEY: Census Number Name Sex Age at Last Birthday Tribe (Seminole, unless otherwise stated) Degree of Blood Marital Status Relationship to Head of Family At Jurisdiction where enrolled [Yes or No] (If no, Where) Ward [Yes or No] Allotment, Annuity, and Identification Numbers (if given).

JIM

226	Billie	m	41	F	m	Head	yes	no
227	Unknown	f	38	F	m	wife	yes	no
228	Unknown	f	11	F	s	dau	yes	no
229	Unknown	f	8	F	s	dau	yes	no
230	Unknown	f	6	F	s	dau	yes	no

| 231 | Frank | m | 30 | F | s | Head | yes | no |

232	Lazy	m	35	F	m	Head	yes	no
233	Mon-ta-kee	f	29	F	m	wife	yes	no
234	Unknown	f	13	F	s	dau	yes	no
235	Unknown	f	12	F	s	dau	yes	no
236	Ah-po-kee	f	18	F	s	niece	yes	no

| 237 | Miami | m | 89 | F | w | Head | yes | no |
| 238 | Jose | m | 36 | F | s | son | yes | no |

239	Webb	m	34	F	m	Head	yes	no
240	Unknown	f	29	F	m	wife	yes	no
241	Unknown	m	12	F	s	son	yes	no
242	Unknown	m	10	F	s	son	yes	no
243	Unknown	f	8	F	s	dau	yes	no
244	Unknown	f	5	F	s	dau	yes	no

| 245 | Willie | m | 33 | F | m | Head | yes | no |
| 246 | Unknown | f | 20 | F | m | wife | yes | no |

JIMMIE

247	Little	m	31	F	m	Head	yes	no
248	Unknown	f	29	F	m	wife	yes	no
249	Unknown	f	13	F	s	dau	yes	no
250	Unknown	m	11	F	s	son	yes	no

Florida Seminoles Indian Census (As of April 1, 1931)

KEY: Census Number Name Sex Age at Last Birthday Tribe (Seminole, unless otherwise stated) Degree of Blood Marital Status Relationship to Head of Family At Jurisdiction where enrolled [Yes or No] (If no, Where) Ward [Yes or No] Allotment, Annuity, and Identification Numbers (if given).

JOHNNY

251	Kir-kee m 36 F s Head yes no
252	Sar-pi-kul-ker f 40 F s sis yes no
253	Ma-har f 38 F s sis yes no

JOHNS

| 254 | Ernie f 43 F s Head yes no |

255	Willie 60 59 F m Head yes no
256	Anne f 65 F m wife yes no
257	Fik-heth-lee f 33 F s dau yes no
258	Oscar m 29 F s son yes no
259	Unknown f 27 F s dau yes no
260	Unknown f 25 F s dau yes no
261	Mok-har-po-kee f 23 F s dau yes no
262	Sac-chee-wah m 21 F s son yes no
263	Ka-see-ha-chee f 19 F s dau yes no
264	Ar-nah f 17 F s dau yes no
265	In-kar-pak-kee m 15 F s son yes no
266	Lizzie f 12 F s dau yes no
267	Unknown f 10 F s dau yes no
268	Unknown f 1 F s grnd-dau yes no

JONES

269	Sam m 37 F m Head yes no
270	Missie Stick f 35 F m wife yes no
271	Free f 17 F s dau yes no
272	Willie m 14 F s son yes no
273	Unknown m 11 F s son yes no
274	Unknown f 9 F s dau yes no
275	Unknown f 7 F s dau yes no
276	Unknown f 5 F s dau yes no
277	Unknown f 3 F s dau yes no
278	Unknown m 2 F s son yes no
279	Sam m 81 F w cousin yes no

Florida Seminoles Indian Census (As of April 1, 1931)

KEY: Census Number Name Sex Age at Last Birthday Tribe (Seminole, unless otherwise stated) Degree of Blood Marital Status Relationship to Head of Family At Jurisdiction where enrolled [Yes or No] (If no, Where) Ward [Yes or No] Allotment, Annuity, and Identification Numbers (if given).

JOSH

280   John m 22 ¼ s Head yes no

JUMPER

281   Mrs. Squirrel f 51 F w Head yes no
282   Stem-i-he-ooh f 31 F s dau yes no
283   Unknown m 28 F s son yes no

284   Charlie m 66 F m Head yes no
285   Wa-to-kee f 58 F m Head yes no
286   Boy m 28 F s stp-son yes no
287   Buffalo Bill m 25 F s stp-son yes no

288   Charlie Knight m 22 F m Head yes no
289   Alice f 16 F m wife yes no

290   Cooter m 44 F m Head yes no
291   Unknown m[sic] 51 F m wife yes no
292   Unknown m 39 F s stp-son yes no
293   Miami Charlie m 29 F s son yes no
294   Unknown f 24 F s dau yes no
295   Unknown f 22 F s dau yes no

296   John Joy m 26 F s Head yes no
297   Figi f 56 F w mother yes no

298   Jose m 26 F m Head yes no
299   Katie f 25 F m wife yes no
300   Moses m 4 F s son yes no

301   Charlie Knight m 49 F m Head yes no
302   Sally f 40 F m wife yes no
303   Unknown m 20 F s son yes no
304   Unknown f 17 F s dau yes no
305   Holly[sic] m 15 F s son yes no
306   Ruby f 13 F s dau yes no

32

Florida Seminoles Indian Census (As of April 1, 1931)

KEY: Census Number Name Sex Age at Last Birthday Tribe (Seminole, unless otherwise stated) Degree of Blood Marital Status Relationship to Head of Family At Jurisdiction where enrolled [Yes or No] (If no, Where) Ward [Yes or No] Allotment, Annuity, and Identification Numbers (if given).

307 Unknown f 9 F s dau yes no

308 Willie m 61 F s Head yes no

McKINLEY

309 William m 36 F m Head yes no
310 To-wee f 29 F m wife yes no
311 Homer m 14 F s son yes no
312 Mitty f 12 F s dau yes no
313 Dixie[sic] m 10 F s son yes no
314 Douglas m 7 F s son yes no
315 Unknown m 4 F s son yes no
316 Unknown m 4/12 F s son yes no

MICCO

317 Charlie m 39 F m Head yes no
318 Was-wah-kee f 31 F m wife yes no
319 Sa-ke-lat-kee f 16 F s dau yes no
320 Unknown f 14 F s dau yes no
321 Unknown f 12 F s dau yes no
322 Unknown f 10 F s dau yes no
323 To-tho-po-ho-chee m 7 F s son yes no
324 Little Jack m 2 F s son yes no

325 Oscar m 3433 F m Head yes no
326 To-chee f 31 F m wife yes no
327 Unknown f 13 F s dau yes no
328 Unknown f 11 F s dau yes no
329 Unknown f 9 F s dau yes no
330 Unknown f 7 F s dau yes no
331 Unknown m 5 F s son yes no

MORGAN

332 Eli m 37 F s Head yes no
333 Unknown f 71 F w mother yes no

33

Florida Seminoles Indian Census (As of April 1, 1931)

KEY: Census Number Name Sex Age at Last Birthday Tribe (Seminole, unless otherwise stated) Degree of Blood Marital Status Relationship to Head of Family At Jurisdiction where enrolled [Yes or No] (If no, Where) Ward [Yes or No] Allotment, Annuity, and Identification Numbers (if given).

334   Jake m 35 F s bro yes no
335   Ma-ma f 26 F s sis yes no
336   **Milliard, Sheela Johns** f 33 F w sis yes no

MOTLOE

337   Jack m 37 F m Head yes no
338   Belle f 35 F m wife yes no
339   Ollie f 5 F s stp-dau yes no

340   John m 31 F s Head yes no
341   Jennie f 46 F w cousin yes no

OSCEOLA

342   Billie m 39 F m Head yes no
343   Ruby f 35 F m wife yes no
344   Tak-hat-a-see f 20 F s dau yes no
345   Unknown f 17 F s dau yes no
346   Che-ho-kee m 15 F s son yes no
347   Unknown f 13 F s dau yes no
348   Unknown m 11 F s son yes no
349   Unknown m 9 F s son yes no
350   Jimmie m 7 F s son yes no

351   Billy m 41 F m Head yes no
352   Unknown f ? F s dau yes no
353   Unknown f 11 F s dau yes no
354   Unknown m 9 F s son yes no

355   Charlie m 24 F m Head yes no
356   Tommie Hand f 32 F m wife yes no
357   Unknown m 4 F s son yes no
358   Unknown f 3 F s dau yes no
359   Unknown f 8/12 F s dau yes no

360   Cori m 26 F m Head yes no
361   Juanita f 22 F m wife yes no

Florida Seminoles Indian Census (As of April 1, 1931)

KEY: Census Number Name Sex Age at Last Birthday Tribe (Seminole, unless otherwise stated) Degree of Blood Marital Status Relationship to Head of Family At Jurisdiction where enrolled [Yes or No] (If no, Where) Ward [Yes or No] Allotment, Annuity, and Identification Numbers (if given).

| 362 | Unknown f 2 F s dau yes no |
| 363 | Unknown m 2/12 F s son yes no |

364	George m 51 F m Head yes no
365	Non-for-me f 40 F m wife yes no
366	Ba-sof-tee m 17 F s son yes no
367	William Buck m 12 F s son yes no
368	Unknown f 11 F s dau yes no
369	Jim-joy m 37 F m Head yes no
370	Unknown f 34 F m wife yes no
371	Unknown f 18 F s dau yes no
372	Unknown f 16 F s dau yes no
373	Unknown m 12 F s son yes no

374	Jimmie m 83 F w Head yes no
375	Sar-ho-kee-see m 18 F s son yes no
376	Lizzie f 16 F s dau yes no
377	Stuman m 14 F s son yes no
378	Richard m 12 F s son yes no

379	John m 61 F m Head yes no
380	Chaw-see f 51 F m wife yes no
381	Unknown f 20 F s dau yes no
382	Te-ki-kee f 16 F s dau yes no
383	Loc-kee m 14 F s son yes no
384	Wah-tee f 12 F s dau yes no
385	Unknown f 7 F s dau yes no

386	John m 49 F m Head yes no
387	Unknown f 49 F m wife yes no
388	Unknown f 26 F s dau yes no
389	Unknown f 23 F s dau yes no
390	Unknown f 21 F s dau yes no
391	Pal-i-kee m 14 F s son yes no

392	Robert m 19 F m Head yes no
393	Unknown f 19 F m wife yes no
394	Roy Nash m 3/12 F s son yes no

35

Florida Seminoles Indian Census (As of April 1, 1931)

KEY: Census Number Name Sex Age at Last Birthday Tribe (Seminole, unless otherwise stated) Degree of Blood Marital Status Relationship to Head of Family At Jurisdiction where enrolled [Yes or No] (If no, Where) Ward [Yes or No] Allotment, Annuity, and Identification Numbers (if given).

395 Wit-kee f 39 F w Head yes no
396 Unknown f 22 F s dau yes no

PARKER

397 Argyl m 31 F s Head yes no
398 Amelia f 35 F s sis yes no

399 Dan m 37 F m Head yes no
400 Unknown f 32 F m wife yes no
401 Unknown f 10 F s stp-dau yes no
402 Unknown m 9 F s stp-son yes no

PEACOCK

403 Charlie m 36 F s Head yes no

PLATT

404 Josh m 27 ¼ s Head yes no
405 Fi-kee f 69 ¼ w mother yes no

PRETTY

406 Old f 63 F w Head yes no

ROBERTS

407 Kar-nac-tee f 23 F s Head yes no
408 To-pi-kee f 21 F s sis yes no
409 Nat-cho-kee m 15 F s bro yes no
410 Lak-kee m 12 F s bro yes no

SMITH

411 Billie m 81 F m Head yes no
412 Mut-to-lo-kee f 76 F m wife yes no
413 Dolly f 48 F s dau yes no

36

Florida Seminoles Indian Census (As of April 1, 1931)

KEY: Census Number Name Sex Age at Last Birthday Tribe (Seminole, unless otherwise stated) Degree of Blood Marital Status Relationship to Head of Family At Jurisdiction where enrolled [Yes or No] (If no, Where) Ward [Yes or No] Allotment, Annuity, and Identification Numbers (if given).

414	Dick m 50 F m Head yes no	
415	Hon-kee f 46 F m wife yes no	
416	Unknown m 15 F s son yes no	
417	Lobie f 14 F s dau yes no	
418	Wa-chee m 9 F s son yes no	

414 Dick m 50 F m Head yes no
415 Hon-kee f 46 F m wife yes no
416 Unknown m 15 F s son yes no
417 Lobie f 14 F s dau yes no
418 Wa-chee m 9 F s son yes no

419 Morgan m 31 F m Head yes no
420 Unknown f 26 F m wife yes no
421 Unknown f 1 F s dau yes no
422 Unknown f 7/12 F s dau yes no

423 Tom m 41 F m Head yes no
424 Stella f 30 F m wife yes no
425 Unknown f 3 F s dau yes no
426 Unknown f 1 F s dau yes no
427 Cully f 32 F s sis yes no

SNOW

428 Samson m 35 F m Head yes no
429 Co-pic-cha-ho-lee f 30 F m wife yes no
430 Chat-lah-nok-kee f 2 F s dau yes no

STEWART

431 Billie m 56 F m Head yes no
432 Susie f 52 f m wife yes no
433 Fannie f 29 F s dau yes no
434 Am-a-chee f 91 F w mother yes no
435 **Charlie, Big** m 48 F s bro-in-law yes no
436 **Snow, Charlie** m 35 F s nephew yes no
437 **Stewart, Mar-po-hat-chee** f 24 F s niece yes no
438 **Wells, Ben** m 22 F s nephew yes no

TIGER

439 Brown m 41 F w Head yes no

Florida Seminoles Indian Census (As of April 1, 1931)

KEY: Census Number Name Sex Age at Last Birthday Tribe (Seminole, unless otherwise stated) Degree of Blood Marital Status Relationship to Head of Family At Jurisdiction where enrolled [Yes or No] (If no, Where) Ward [Yes or No] Allotment, Annuity, and Identification Numbers (if given).

440   Charlie m 49 F w Head yes no

441   Cuffney m 52 F m Head yes no
442   Unknown f 50 F m wife yes no
443   Unknown f 8 F s dau yes no
444   Doctor m 52 F w Head yes no

445   Emma f 40 F w Head yes no
446   Unknown f 21 F s dau yes no
447   Unknown m 19 F s son yes no

448   Frank m 40 F w Head yes no
449   John Frank m 20 F s son yes no
450   Unknown f 18 F s dau yes no
451   Unknown f 16 F s dau yes no
452   Unknown f 14 F s dau yes no
453   Unknown m 12 F s son yes no

454   Jim m 49 F m Head yes no
455   Unknown f 59 F m wife yes no
456   Little m 28 F s son yes no
457   Unknown f 26 F s dau yes no
458   Unknown m 23 F s son yes no
459   Unknown m 19 F s son yes no

460   Miami John m 54 F m Head yes no
461   Unknown f 45 F m wife yes no
462   Unknown m 23 F s son yes no
463   Unknown m 19 F s son yes no
464   Unknown m 17 F s son yes no
465   Unknown f 15 F s dau yes no
466   Willie m 61 F w bro-in-law yes no
467   **Billie, Homespun** m 40 F s bro-in-law yes no

468   Nac-o-tee f 38 F w Head yes no
469   Unknown m 21 F s son yes no
470   Unknown f 17 F s dau yes no
471   Unknown m 15 F s son yes no

Florida Seminoles Indian Census (As of April 1, 1931)

KEY: Census Number Name Sex Age at Last Birthday Tribe (Seminole, unless otherwise stated) Degree of Blood Marital Status Relationship to Head of Family At Jurisdiction where enrolled [Yes or No] (If no, Where) Ward [Yes or No] Allotment, Annuity, and Identification Numbers (if given).

472 Unknown f 13 F s dau yes no

473 Na-ha m 45 F m Head yes no
474 Lucy f 53 F m wife yes no

475 San-tee m 29 F s Head yes no

476 Tiger m 36 F m Head yes no
477 Ruby f 33 F m wife yes no
478 Tiger Boy m 16 F s son yes no
479 Mar-stook-kee f 14 F s dau yes no
480 Frank m 12 F s son yes no
481 Josie m 10 F s son yes no
482 Cypress m 8 F s son yes no
483 Harjo m 6 F s son yes no
484 Unknown f 4 F s dau yes no
485 Unknown f 6/12 F s dau yes no

TIGERTAIL

486 Charlic m 61 F w Head yes no
487 Cat-ath-lee m 15 F s son yes no
488 Lofton m 21 F m Head yes no
489 Na-ha-we f 18 F m wife yes no
490 Doc Wilson m 27 F s half-bro yes no
491 Unknown f 25 F s half-sis yes no
492 Edna f 17 F s sis yes no
493 Unknown f 15 F s sis yes no
494 Unknown f 13 F s sis yes no
495 Unknown f 10 F s sis yes no

TOMMIE

496 Anna f 75 F w Head yes no
497 Annie May f 38 F s dau yes no
498 Brownie m 32 f s son yes no
499 Tony m 31 F w son yes no

Florida Seminoles Indian Census (As of April 1, 1931)

KEY: Census Number Name Sex Age at Last Birthday Tribe (Seminole, unless otherwise stated) Degree of Blood Marital Status Relationship to Head of Family At Jurisdiction where enrolled [Yes or No] (If no, Where) Ward [Yes or No] Allotment, Annuity, and Identification Numbers (if given).

500	Ben F m 48 F m Head yes no
501	Tudle f 36 F m wife yes no
502	Mary f 9 F s dau yes no
503	**Tiger, Missie** f 43 F s sis-in-law yes no
504	**Parker, Mary** f 9 F s niece yes no
505	**Parker, Agnes** f 7 F s niece yes no
506	Charlie m 58 F s Head yes no
507	Charlie m 57 F m Head yes no
508	Cho-bee f 53 F m wife yes no
509	Frank m 35 F m Head yes no
510	Ho-mi-pee f 25 F m wife yes no
511	Willie Micco m 4 F s son yes no
512	Es-tah-kah-yee m 1 F s son yes no
513	Jack m 3 F m Head yes no
514	Unknown f 26 F m wife yes no
515	Unknown m 1 F s son yes no
516	Unknown m 9 F s son yes no
517	Unknown m 7 F s son yes no
518	Unknown f 6 F s dau yes no
519	Unknown m 4 F s son yes no
520	Herbert Hoover m 2 F s son yes no
521	Unknown m 4/12 F s son yes no
522	**Billie, Willie** m 41 F w bro-in-law yes no
523	Jim m 35 F m Head yes no
524	Lo-bee f 28 m wife yes no
525	Unknown m 4 F s son yes no
526	Lody f 27 s Head yes no
527	Morgan Baby f 6 F s dau yes no
528	Sam m 26 F m Head yes no
529	Melid f 17 F m wife yes no
530	Unknown m 2/12 F s son yes no

40

Florida Seminoles Indian Census (As of April 1, 1931)

KEY: Census Number Name Sex Age at Last Birthday Tribe (Seminole, unless otherwise stated) Degree of Blood Marital Status Relationship to Head of Family At Jurisdiction where enrolled [Yes or No] (If no, Where) Ward [Yes or No] Allotment, Annuity, and Identification Numbers (if given).

531 Small –pox m 44 F m Head yes no
532 Mary f 36 F m wife yes no

TONY

533 Young m 49 F m Head yes no
534 Unknown f 43 F m wife yes no
535 Sim-pa-ha-ke f 18 F s dau yes no
536 Cla-sa-ho-yee f 12 F s dau yes
537 Jimmie Billie m 31 F s nephew yes no
538 Unknown m 29 F s nephew yes no
539 Unknown f 26 F s niece yes no
540 Jimmie Doctor f[sic] 24 F s nephew yes no

TUCKER

541 Chaw-huc-kee f 70 F w Head yes no
542 Ho-po-thut-kee f 53 F s dau yes no
543 Mait-kah f 50 F s dau yes no
544 Sar-thler-nalı-kce f 27 F dau yes no
545 Frank m 25 F s son yes no
546 Nok-me-lee-kee m 25 F s grnd-son yes no
547 Te-heth-lee-kee f 24 F s grnd-dau yes no

548 Oscar m 35 F m Head yes no
549 Cot-ner f 32 F m wife yes no
550 Cus-sum-lak-chee f 16 F s dau yes no
551 Unknown m 13 F s son yes no
552 Unknown m 10 F s son yes no
553 Unknown m 7 F s son yes no

WALKER

554 Henry m 63 F m Head yes no
555 Unknown f 51 F m wife yes no
556 Unknown f 27 F s dau yes no

557 Wat-cha-kee m 28 F s Head yes no

Florida Seminoles Indian Census (As of April 1, 1931)

KEY: Census Number Name Sex Age at Last Birthday Tribe (Seminole, unless otherwise stated) Degree of Blood Marital Status Relationship to Head of Family At Jurisdiction where enrolled [Yes or No] (If no, Where) Ward [Yes or No] Allotment, Annuity, and Identification Numbers (if given).

WILLIE

558 Frank m 46 F w Head yes no
559 O-mas-kee m 14 F s son yes no
560 Yo-pote-ama f 12 F s dau yes no

561 Jesse m 31 F m Head yes no
562 Unknown f 28 F m wife yes no
563 Unknown f 11 F s dau yes no
564 Unknown f 10 F s dau yes no

565 Johnny m 61 F w Head yes no

566 Sam m 39 F m Head yes no
567 Unknown f 31 F m wife yes no
568 Henry m 12 F s son yes no
569 Walter Roy m 9 F s son yes no
570 Mary f 6 F s dau yes no
571 Unknown m 4 F s son yes no
572 **Charlie, Corinne** f 25 F w sis-in-law yes no
573 **Charlie, Pauline** f 5 F s niece yes no

WILSON

574 Ben m 27 F s Head yes no
575 Unknown f 16 F s sis yes no

Florida Seminoles Indian Census (As of April 1, 1931)

KEY: Census Number Name Sex Age at Last Birthday Tribe (Seminole, unless otherwise stated) Degree of Blood Marital Status Relationship to Head of Family At Jurisdiction where enrolled [Yes or No] (If no, Where) Ward [Yes or No] Allotment, Annuity, and Identification Numbers (if given).

DEDUCTIONS
(Dropped – (Reason unknown)
(Number is **last census** roll number)

BILLIE

27	Suc-a-to-yee f 26 F s dau yes no
29	Ruby f 22 F s dau yes no
30	La-ke-kee m 18 F s son yes no

BILLY

| 72 | Belle f 24 F m wife yes no |
| 73 | Unknown m 2 F s son yes no |

DOCTOR

| 171 | Unknown ·f 15 F s dau yes no |
| 172 | Unknown f 13 F s dau yes no |

FEWELL

| 189 | Le-to-kee f 24 F s dau yes no |

HALLS

| 219 | Oscar m 69 F s Head yes no |

TIGER

| 435 | Unknown m 7 F s son yes no |

TIGERTAIL

| 482 | Wilson m 18 F m Head yes no |

TOMMIE

Florida Seminoles Indian Census (As of April 1, 1931)

KEY: Census Number Name Sex Age at Last Birthday Tribe (Seminole, unless otherwise stated) Degree of Blood Marital Status Relationship to Head of Family At Jurisdiction where enrolled [Yes or No] (If no, Where) Ward [Yes or No] Allotment, Annuity, and Identification Numbers (if given).

521   Jimmie m 34 F m Head yes no
522   Unknown f 35 F m wife yes no
523   Unknown m 4 F s son yes no

TUCKER

540   Susie f 28 F m wife yes no

DEATHS
(Number is **last census** roll number)

BILLY

57   Unknown m 15 F s son yes no
58   Unknown m 13 F s son yes no
59   Unknown f 11 F s dau yes no

62   Unknown m 4/12 F s son yes no

70   Miami m 93 F w Head yes no

DOCTOR

169   John m 69 F m Head yes no
181   Dorsie f 4 F s dau yes no

FRAZIER

201   Mon-o-la-kee f 21 F m wife yes no

GOPHER

204   Coffee m 45 F m Head yes no

Florida Seminoles Indian Census (As of April 1, 1931)

KEY: Census Number Name Sex Age at Last Birthday Tribe (Seminole, unless otherwise stated) Degree of Blood Marital Status Relationship to Head of Family At Jurisdiction where enrolled [Yes or No] (If no, Where) Ward [Yes or No] Allotment, Annuity, and Identification Numbers (if given).

OSCEOLA

353   Mary f 37 F m wife yes no

359   Unknown f 5 F s dau yes no

TIGER

432   Unknown f 12 F s son yes no
433   Unknown m 9 F s son yes no

TOMMIE

500   Charlie m 50 F w Head yes no

517   **Chippo, Emma** f 69 F w mother-in-law yes no

TUCKER

539   Bill m 49 F m Head yes no

WILLIE

572   John m 7 F s son yes no

WILSON

578   Yu-pak-lat-kah m 53 F w father yes no

Births (Between July 1, 1924, and March 31, 1931)

KEY: Census Number and Year Given Name of Parent (Baby's Name) Birthdate Sex Tribe (Seminole, unless otherwise stated) Ward [Yes or No] Degree of Father's Blood Degree of Mother's Blood Degree of Child's Blood At Jurisdiction where enrolled [Yes or No] (If no, Where).

July 1, 1924 thru June 30, 1925

7   1927   Billie, Carney *(No name)* 1925 m yes F F F yes

143   1927   Doctor, Hal (Co-sop-cho-tee) 1924 f yes F F F yes

158   1927   Doctor, Little *(No name)* 1924 f yes F F F yes

209   1927   Jim, Billie *(No name)* 1924 f yes F F F yes

271   1927   McKinley, William (Douglass) 1924 m yes F F F yes

279   1927   Micco, Charley (To-the-po-ho-chee) 11-1924 f yes F F F yes

293   1928   Osceola, Billie *(No name)* 1924 m yes F F F yes

288   1929   Osceola, Charley *(No name)* 1925 f yes F F F yes

412   1927   Tiger, Tiger *(No name)* 1925 m yes F F F yes

182   1926   Tiger, Ada (Howard) 1925 m yes W F F yes

182   1925   Tiger, Missie (Agnes) 1925 f yes F F F yes

445   1927   Tommie, Jack (Unknown) 1925 f yes F F F yes

515   1929   Tommie, Lady (Morgan Baby) 1925 f yes F F F yes

498   1927   Willie, Sam (Mary) 1925 f yes F F F yes

July 1, 1925 thru June 30, 1926

18   1927   Billie, Philip (John Philip) 1926 m yes F F F yes

53   1927   Billie, Josie *(No name)* 1926 f yes F F F yes

144   1927   Doctor, Hal (She-cho-pee) 1926 m yes F F F yes

46

Births (Between July 1, 1924, and March 31, 1931)

KEY: Census Number and Year Given Name of Parent (Baby's Name) Birthdate Sex Tribe (Seminole, unless otherwise stated) Ward [Yes or No] Degree of Father's Blood Degree of Mother's Blood Degree of Child's Blood At Jurisdiction where enrolled [Yes or No] (If no, Where).

159 1927 Doctor, Little (Dorsie) 1926 f yes F F F yes

172 1927 Fewell, John (Juanita) 1926 F yes F F F yes

225 1927 Jim, Webb *(No name)* 1926 f yes F F F yes

288 1927 Motloe, Jack (Ollie) 1926 f yes F F F yes

491 1927 Willie, Jessie *(No name)* 1926 f yes F F F yes

121 1930 Cypress, Charley (Tomafinp)[sic] 1926 f yes F F F yes

108 1930 Charlie, Corinne (Pauline) 1926 f yes F F F yes

274 1930 Jones, Sam (Unknown) 1926 f yes F F F yes

326 1930 Micco, Oscar (Unknown) 1926 m yes F F F yes

July 1, 1926 thru June 30, 1927

8 1927 Billie, Carney *(No name)* 1927 f yes F F F yes

55 1928 Billie, Josie *(No name)* 1927 m yes F F F yes

172 1928 Frazier, Bird *(No name)* 1927 m yes F F F yes

255 1927 Jumper, Josie (Moses) 5-20-1927 m yes F F F yes

272 1927 McKinley, Wm *(No name)* 1927 m yes F F F yes

289 1929 Osceola, Charley *(No name)* 1927 m yes F F F yes

415 1930 Smith, Tom *(No name)* 1927 f yes F F F yes

439 1927 Tommie, Frank (Willie Micco) 1927 m yes F F F yes
446 1927 Tommie, Jack *(No name)* 1927 m yes F F F yes

449 1927 Tommie, Jim *(No name)* 1927 m yes F F F yes

47

Births (Between July 1, 1924, and March 31, 1931)

KEY: Census Number and Year Given Name of Parent (Baby's Name) Birthdate Sex Tribe (Seminole, unless otherwise stated) Ward [Yes or No] Degree of Father's Blood Degree of Mother's Blood Degree of Child's Blood At Jurisdiction where enrolled [Yes or No] (If no, Where).

July 1, 1927 thru June 30, 1928

47   1929   Billie, John *(No name)* 4-1928 f yes F F F yes

58   1929   Billie, Robert *(No name)* 1928 m yes F F F yes

507   1929   Billie, Yarber *(No name)* 1928 m yes F F F yes

103   1930   Buster, Johnny (2) *(No name)* 1927 latter half m yes F F F yes

100   1929   Cypress, Charley (Stanley Hanson) 1-1928 m yes F F F yes

130   1930   Cypress, Johnny *(No name)* 1-1928 m yes F F F yes

191   1929   Huff, Pocahontas (George) 11-9-1928 m yes F F F yes

290   1929   Osceola, Charley *(No name)* 11-9-1928 f yes F F F yes

415   1928   Tiger, Tiger *(No name)* 11-9-1928 f yes F F F yes

502   1928   Willie, Sam *(No name)* 1927 latter half m yes F F F yes

275   1930   Jones, Sam *(No name)* 1928 f yes F F F yes

July 1, 1928 thru June 30, 1929

106   1930   Buster, Johnny (2) (Unknown) 1929 m yes F F F yes

124   1930   Cypress, Charley (Unknown) 1929 f yes F F F yes

276   1930   Jones, Sam (Unknown) 1929 m yes F F F yes
325   1930   Micco, Charley (Little Jack) 1929 m yes F F F yes

412   1930   Smith, Morgan (Unknown) 1929 f yes F F F yes

Births (Between July 1, 1924, and March 31, 1931)

KEY: Census Number and Year Given Name of Parent (Baby's Name) Birthdate Sex Tribe (Seminole, unless otherwise stated) Ward [Yes or No] Degree of Father's Blood Degree of Mother's Blood Degree of Child's Blood At Jurisdiction where enrolled [Yes or No] (If no, Where).

442 1929 Tommie, Jack (Herbert Hoover) 8-12-1928 f yes F F F yes

560 1930 Willie, Frank (Little) 1-5-1929 f yes F F F yes

416 1930 Smith, Tom (Unknown) 1929 f yes F F F yes

July 1, 1929 thru June 30, 1930

7 1930 Billie, Suc-a-to-yee (Unknown) 1930 f yes F F F yes

21 1930 Billie, Kunzie (Unknown) 1930 f yes F F F yes

157 1930 Doctor, Cologne (Unknown) 10-1929 f yes F F F yes

162 1930 Doctor, Grover (Unknown) 10-1929 m yes F F F yes

200 1930 Frazier, Bird (Unknown) 10-22-1929 m yes F F F yes

209 1930 Gopher, Coffee's Dau (Unknown) 1930 f yes F F F yes

266 1930 Johns, Oscar (Unknown) 10-1929 f yes F F F yes

357 1930 Osceola, Cori (Unknown) 6-19-1929 m yes F F F yes

423 1930 Snow, Samson (Chat-lah-nok-kee) 8-1929 f yes F F F yes

507 1930 Tommie, Frank (Es-tah-kah-yee) 12-22-1929 m yes F F F yes

355 1929 Tiger, *(blank)* (Tonetta) 1-21-1929 *(No other information given)*

April 1, 1930 thru March 31, 1931

Not enrolled Jim, Willie (Unknown) 1-16-1931 f yes F F F yes

316 1931 McKinley, Wm (Unknown) 12-1930 m yes F F F yes

49

Births (Between July 1, 1924, and March 31, 1931)

359   1931   Osceola, Charley (Unknown) 8-1930 f yes F F F yes

363   1931   Osceola, Cori (Unknown) 2-12-1931 m yes F F F yes

394   1931   Osceola, Robert (Roy Nash) 1-1931 m yes F F F yes

422   1931   Smith, Morgan (Unknown) 8-9-1930 f yes F F F yes

485   1931   Tiger, Tiger (Unknown) 9-1930 f yes F F F yes

521   1931   Tommie, Jack (Unknown) 12-1930 m yes F F F yes

530   1931   Tommie, Sam (Unknown) 1-1931 m yes F F F yes

Deaths (Between July 1, 1924, and March 31, 1931)

KEY: Census Number and Year Name Death Date Age at Death Sex Tribe (Seminole, unless otherwise stated) Ward [Yes or No] Degree of Blood Cause of Death At Jurisdiction where enrolled [Yes or No] (If no, Where).

July 1, 1924 thru June 30, 1925

50	1924	Billy, To-kee 5-30-1925 22 f yes F Unknown yes
60	1926	Buck, Billie 1925 67 m yes F Unknown yes
62	1926	Buck, John's wife 1925 23 f yes ? Unknown yes
121	1926	Dennis, Mister 1925 60 m yes ? Unknown yes
305	1924	Parker, Hattie 8-29-1924 25 f yes ? Unknown yes
450	1924	Willie, Charlie 12-26-1924 69 m yes ? Unknown yes
452	1926	Willie, Frank's wife 1925 28 f yes ? Unknown yes
466	1926	Willie, Sallie 1925 60 f yes ? Unknown yes

July 1, 1926 thru June 30, 1927

25	1927	Billie, Tim-shee 1927 45 f yes F Unknown ?
21	1927	Bowers, Hattie 1927 21 f yes F Unknown ?
83	1926	Chippo, Tallahassee 1926 65 m yes F Unknown ?
92	1926	Conepatchie, Billie 1926 69 m yes F Unknown ?
195	1927	Hillard, John 1927 34 m yes F Unknown ?
252	1927	Jumper, Cooter's dau 1927 9 f yes F Unknown ?
368	1927	Tiger, Bessie 1927 35 f yes F Unknown ?
496	1927	Willie, Archie 1927 6 m yes F Unknown ?
457	1926	Willie, Jim 1926 29 m yes F Unknown ?

51

Deaths (Between July 1, 1924, and March 31, 1931)

KEY: Census Number and Year Name Death Date Age at Death Sex Tribe (Seminole, unless otherwise stated) Ward [Yes or No] Degree of Blood Cause of Death At Jurisdiction where enrolled [Yes or No] (If no, Where).

458   1926   Willie, Jim s wife 1926 24 f yes F Unknown ?

July 1, 1927 thru June 30, 1928

312   1927   Osceola, Am-su-sie 3-1928 34 f yes F Unknown ?

366   1927   Tiger, Sem-o-kee 1927 24 f yes F Unknown ?

381   1928   Tiger, Mot-see 6-1-1928 58 f yes F Unknown ?

370   1927   Tiger, Cypress 1928 33 m yes F Unknown ?

382   1927   Tiger, Cat-see 1927 34 f yes F Unknown ?

453   1927   Tommy, Edna John 2-17-1928 22 f yes TB ?

Not on Roll   Billy, Martin John 5-7-1928 ? m yes F Unknown ?

July 1, 1928 thru June 30, 1929

1   1928   Billie, Carney 5-14-1928 31 m yes F Drowning ?

23   1928   Billie, Kowchia 5-29-1929 5 m yes F Oemebic dysentery ?

79   1928   Buster, Jack 3-9-1929 49 m yes F Gun shot ?

154   1929   Doctor, Tommie's wife 1928 50 f yes F Unknown ?

92   1928   Clay, Charlie Lee 2-20-1929 27 m yes F Knife wound ?

97   1928   Conepatchie, Nancy 1-26-1929 59 f yes F Influenza ?

101   1927   Cypress, Charlie's dau 12-1928 20 f yes F Unknown ?

335   1928   Roberts, Nuf-kee 12-16-1928 38 f yes F Knife wound ?

417   1928   Tiger, Lucy 12-7-1928 56 f yes F Unknown ?

Deaths (Between July 1, 1924, and March 31, 1931)

KEY: Census Number and Year Name Death Date Age at Death Sex Tribe (Seminole, unless otherwise stated) Ward [Yes or No] Degree of Blood Cause of Death At Jurisdiction where enrolled [Yes or No] (If no, Where).

358 1929 Tiger, Brown's stp-dau 1928 14 f yes F Unknown ?

498 1929 Willie, Willie 6-28-1929 42 m yes F General peritonitis ?

502 1927 Wilson, Lake 1928 52 m yes F Unknown ?

July 1, 1929 thru June 30, 1930

15 1929 Billie, Philip 1929 23 m yes F Unknown ?

44 1929 Billie, John's wife 1929 79 f yes F Old age ?

85 1929 Charlie, Frank 8-15-1929 29 m yes F
                              Drowning by auto wreck ?

204 1930 Gopher, Coffee 6-1-1930 45 m yes F TB ?

312 1929 Osceola, Charlie 8-15-1929 22 m yes F
                              Drowning by auto wreck ?

364 1929 Tiger, Par-to-kee 1929 47 f yes F Unknown ?

386 1929 Tiger, Little's wife 1929 82 f yes F Old age ?

413 1929 Tigertail, Jack's wife 8-15-1929 44 f yes F
                              Drowning by auto wreck ?

427 1929 Tommie, Charlie's wife 1929 28 f yes F Unknown ?

572 1930 Willie, John 6-8-1930 7 m yes F Unknown ?

555 1929 Tiger, Tonette 3-1-1930 1 f yes F Unknown ?

April 1, 1930 thru March 31, 1931

57 1930 Billie, John's son 1930 15 m yes F Unknown ?

Deaths (Between July 1, 1924, and March 31, 1931)

KEY: Census Number and Year Name Death Date Age at Death Sex Tribe (Seminole, unless otherwise stated) Ward [Yes or No] Degree of Blood Cause of Death At Jurisdiction where enrolled [Yes or No] (If no, Where).

58	1930	Billy, John's son 1930 13 m yes F Unknown ?
59	1930	Billy, John's dau 1930 11 f yes F Unknown ?
70	1930	Billy, Miami 1930 93 m yes F Old age ?
169	1930	Doctor, John 1930 69 m yes F Unknown ?
181	1930	Doctor, Dorsie 12-1930 4 f yes F Unknown ?
201	1930	Frazier, Mon-o-la-kee 8-4-1930 21 f yes F Unknown ?
Not on Roll		Jim, Willie's dau 2-14-1931 1 mo f yes F Unknown ?
353	1930	Osceola, Mary 7-20-1930 37 f yes F Unknown ?
359	1930	Osceola, Charlie's stp-dau 9-28-1930 f yes F Unknown ?
432	1930	Tiger, Brown's stp-dau 1931 12 f yes F Unknown ?
433	1930	Tiger, Brown's stp-son 1930 9 m yes F Unknown ?
500	1930	Tommie, Charlie 7-30-1930 50 m yes F Drowning ?
517	1930	Chippo, Emma 12-11-1930 69 f yes F Old age ?

Florida Seminoles Indian Census (As of April 1, 1932)

KEY: Census Number; Name; Sex; Age at Last Birthday; Tribe (Seminole, unless otherwise stated); Degree of Blood; Marital Status; Relationship to Head of Family; At Jurisdiction where enrolled [Yes or No] (If no, Where); Ward [Yes or No]; Allotment, Annuity, and Identification Numbers (if given).

BILLIE

1	[Mrs. Carney] Sac-a-to-yee f 32 F w Head yes yes
2	[Lo-lee] Johnson m 13 F s son yes yes
3	[He-chee] Johnny m 11 F s son yes yes
4	[Ko-ta-kee] Edna f 9 F s dau yes yes
5	Larry m 7 F s son yes yes
6	Minnie f 6 F s dau yes yes
7	Peggy f 1 F s dau yes yes
8	Rosalie f 18 F ? Sis yes yes

9 Charlie m ? F m Head yes yes
10 Emma f ? F m wife yes yes
11 Chestnut m ? F s son yes yes
12 Ruby f 24 F s dau yes yes
13 Maggie m 20 F s dau yes yes

14 Cowboy m 22 F m Head yes yes
15 Annie f 19 F m wife yes yes

16 Girtman m 36 F w Head yes yes
17 Sa-wit-skee m 14 F s son yes yes

18 Kunzie m 36 F m Head yes yes
19 Addie f 33 F m wife yes yes
20 Unknown m 10 F s son yes yes
21 Unknown f 2 F s dau yes yes

22 Little Charlie m 35 F m Head yes yes
23 Chi-ki-kee f 50 F m wife yes yes

24 Mary f 35 F w Head yes yes

25 Willie #1 m 55 F w Head yes yes

26 John m 26 F m Head yes yes
27 Ma-wee-he-lee f 38 F m wife yes yes

55

Florida Seminoles Indian Census (As of April 1, 1932)

KEY: Census Number; Name; Sex; Age at Last Birthday; Tribe (Seminole, unless otherwise stated); Degree of Blood; Marital Status; Relationship to Head of Family; At Jurisdiction where enrolled [Yes or No] (If no, Where); Ward [Yes or No]; Allotment, Annuity, and Identification Numbers (if given).

28   Homer m 5 F s son yes yes

29   Willie #2 m 43 F w Head yes yes
30   Johnny m 18 F s son yes yes
31   George m 14 F s son yes yes
32   Yarber m 25 F m Head yes yes
33   Unknown f 20 F m wife yes yes
34   Unknown m 4 F s son yes yes

35   Grover m 36 F m Head yes yes
36   Unknown f 26 F m wife yes yes
37   Unknown m 15 F s son yes yes
38   Unknown f 13 F s dau yes yes

39   Ingram m 37 F m Head yes yes
40   Tak-ho-kee f 36 F m wife yes yes
41   Johnson m 18 F s son yes yes
42   Unknown m 10 F s son yes yes
43   *(Illegible)* m ? F s son yes yes
44   Edna f 11 F s dau yes yes

45   John #2 87 F m Head yes yes
46   Hah-won-a-ha-yee f 19 F m wife yes yes
47   Effie f 7 F s dau yes yes
48   Unknown f 5 F s dau yes yes

49   Josie m 46 F m Head yes yes
50   Wat-see f 42 F m wife yes yes
51   E-sa-wee f 14 F s dau yes yes
52   Es-sta-vee f 10 F s dau yes yes
53   Li-to-e-kee f 6 F s dau yes yes
54   Sha-he-thee m 5 F s son yes yes

55   Robert m 31 F m Head yes yes
56   Josie f 32 F m wife yes yes
57   Milton m 2 F s son yes yes
58   Wilson m 31 F m Head yes yes

KEY: Census Number; Name; Sex; Age at Last Birthday; Tribe (Seminole, unless otherwise stated); Degree of Blood; Marital Status; Relationship to Head of Family; At Jurisdiction where enrolled [Yes or No] (If no, Where); Ward [Yes or No]; Allotment, Annuity, and Identification Numbers (if given).

BOWLEGS

59	Billy	m	65	¼	w	Head	yes	yes	
60	**Tucker, Lewis**	m	47	¼	s	bro	yes	yes	
61	**Pearce, Lucy**	f	51	F	w	sis	yes	yes	
62	**Pearce, Ada**	f	22	F	s	niece	yes	yes	
63	**Pearce, Anna**	f	20	F	s	niece	yes	yes	

BOWERS

64	Joe	m	53	F	m	Head	yes	yes	
65	Lena	f	33	F	m	wife	yes	yes	
66	Jackson	m	24	F	w	son	yes	yes	
67	Lydee	f	21	F	s	dau	yes	yes	
68	Dick	m	17	F	s	son	yes	yes	
69	Ka-pik-oka-ha-che	m	16	F	s	son	yes	yes	
70	Unknown	m	13	F	s	son	yes	yes	
71	Unknown	m	8	F	s	son	yes	yes	
72	Unknown	m	8	F	s	son	yes	yes	
73	Lillie	f	36	F	w	Head	yes	yes	
74	Tom Buster	m	15	F	s	son	yes	yes	
75	Bessie Buster	f	7	F	s	dau	yes	yes	
76	**Willie, Ruby**	f	41	F	w	sis	yes	yes	
77	**Willie, Little**	f	3	F	s	niece	yes	yes	

BUCK

78	John	m	34	F	w	Head	yes	yes	

BUSTER

79	Billie	m	66	F	m	Head	yes	yes	
80	Nellie	f	81	F	m	wife	yes	yes	
81	Ar-nah	f	63	F	s	stp-dau	yes	yes	
82	Yek-am-kah	f	33	F	s	dau	yes	yes	
83	No-ket-cher	f	33	F	s	dau	yes	yes	

Florida Seminoles Indian Census (As of April 1, 1932)

KEY: Census Number; Name; Sex; Age at Last Birthday; Tribe (Seminole, unless otherwise stated); Degree of Blood; Marital Status; Relationship to Head of Family; At Jurisdiction where enrolled [Yes or No] (If no, Where); Ward [Yes or No]; Allotment, Annuity, and Identification Numbers (if given).

84   Charlie 57 60 F w Head yes yes

85   Po-lah-lee f 52 F w Head yes yes
86   Addie f 33 F m dau yes yes
87   Little f 29 F s dau yes yes
88   Unknown f 25 F s dau yes yes

89   Jo(sic) ? ? F s Head yes yes

90   John m ? F m Head yes yes
91   In-git-tah-yee f ? F m wife yes yes
92   So-wah-ho-yee f ? F s dau yes yes
93   Unknown m ? F s son yes yes
94   Unknown m ? F s son yes yes

CHARLIE

95   Chief m 25 F m Head yes yes
96   Rosalie f 35 F m wife yes yes
97   [Alice] f ? F s stp-dau yes yes

98   Frank m 21 F m Head yes yes
99   [Carrie] f 20 F m wife yes yes

CLAY

100   Ka-ki-kee f 42 F w Head yes yes
101   Abraham Lincoln m 34 F s son yes yes
102   Jack Johnson m 28 F s son yes yes
103   To-li-kee f 26 F s dau yes yes
104   Ta-li-kee f 20 F s dau yes yes
105   Nac-ho-mee f 12 F s dau yes yes

CYPRESS

106   Charlie m 57 F m Head yes yes
107   Lee f 48 F m wife yes yes

58

Florida Seminoles Indian Census (As of April 1, 1932)

KEY: Census Number; Name; Sex; Age at Last Birthday; Tribe (Seminole, unless otherwise stated); Degree of Blood; Marital Status; Relationship to Head of Family; At Jurisdiction where enrolled [Yes or No] (If no, Where); Ward [Yes or No]; Allotment, Annuity, and Identification Numbers (if given).

108	Henry	m	18	F	s	son	yes	yes
109	Tomafino	f	6	F	s	dau	yes	yes
110	Stanley Hanson	m	4	F	s	son	yes	yes

111	Futch	m	62	F	m	Head	yes	yes
112	Unknown	f	45	m	wife	yes	yes
113	Harry	m	25	F	s	son	yes	yes

| 114 | Henry | m | 27 | F | m | Head | yes | yes |
| 115 | *(Illegible)* | f | ? | ? | m | wife | yes | yes |

116	Johnny	m	30	F	m	Head	yes	yes
117	My-ho-chee	f	28	F	m	wife	yes	yes
118	Unknown	m	10	F	s	son	yes	yes
119	Unknown	m	4	F	s	son	yes	yes
120	Unknown	m	10/12	F	s	son	yes	yes

121	Whitney	m	52	F	m	Head	yes	yes
122	Sally	f	40	F	m	wife	yes	yes
123	Suc-la-to-kee	f	18	F	s	dau	yes	yes
124	See-ho-kee	f	16	F	s	dau	yes	yes
125	Look-eet-see	m	13	F	s	son	yes	yes
126	Che-na-see	f	11	F	s	dau	yes	yes
127	Unknown	m	9	F	s	son	yes	yes
128	**Fewell, Billy**	m	93	F	w	father-in-law	yes	yes

129	Wilson	m	44	F	m	Head	yes	yes
130	Ruby	f	34	F	m	wife	yes	yes
131	Unknown	f	16	F	s	dau	yes	yes
132	Unknown	f	15	F	s	dau	yes	yes
133	Unknown	f	14	F	s	dau	yes	yes
134	Unknown	m	9	F	s	son	yes	yes

DIXIE

| 135 | Charlie | m | 60 | ¼ | m | Head | yes | yes |
| 136 | Jim-sling | f | 55 | F | m | wife | yes | yes |

KEY: Census Number; Name; Sex; Age at Last Birthday; Tribe (Seminole, unless otherwise stated); Degree of Blood; Marital Status; Relationship to Head of Family; At Jurisdiction where enrolled [Yes or No] (If no, Where); Ward [Yes or No]; Allotment, Annuity, and Identification Numbers (if given).

137 Walter m 27 ¼ s son yes yes
138 Susie f 22 ¼ s dau yes yes
139 Samson m 10 ¼ s son yes yes
140 Billy, Mrs. Miami f 97 F w mother-in-law yes yes

DOCTOR

141 Cologne m 36 F m Head yes yes
142 Unknown f 31 F m wife yes yes
143 Unknown m 16 F s son yes yes
144 Unknown m 12 F s son yes yes
145 Unknown m 9 F s son yes yes
146 Unknown f 2 F s dau yes yes

147 Nac-o-tee f 33 F w Head yes yes
148 Unknown m 10 F s son yes yes
149 Unknown f 9 F s dau yes yes
150 Unknown m 2 F s son yes yes

151 Hal m 37 F m Head yes yes
152 Annie f 37 F m wife yes yes
153 Lat-i-kee m 14 F s son yes yes
154 Unknown m 12 F s son yes yes
155 Unknown f 10 F s dau yes yes
156 Co-sop-cho-tee m 8 F s son yes yes
157 She-cho-pee m 6 F s son yes yes

158 Unknown f 51 F w Head yes yes
159 Unknown m 13 F s son yes yes
160 Unknown m 11 F s son yes yes
161 Unknown f 9 F s dau yes yes

162 Little m 64 F m Head yes yes
163 Mamie f 36 F m wife yes yes
164 Tommie m 12 F s son yes yes

165 Wilson m 32 F m Head yes yes

KEY: Census Number; Name; Sex; Age at Last Birthday; Tribe (Seminole, unless otherwise stated); Degree of Blood; Marital Status; Relationship to Head of Family; At Jurisdiction where enrolled [Yes or No] (If no, Where); Ward [Yes or No]; Allotment, Annuity, and Identification Numbers (if given).

166   O-sha-fish-shee   f   33   F   m   wife   yes   yes
167   Unknown   m   3   F   s   son   yes   yes

DRUITT

168   Jimmy   m   32   F   m   Head   yes   yes
169   Unknown   f   20   F   m   wife   yes   yes
170   Unknown   f   10   F   s   dau   yes   yes
171   Unknown   m   8   F   s   son   yes   yes
172   Unknown   m   4   F   s   son   yes   yes

FEWELL

173   Charlie   m   56   F   m   Head   yes   yes
174   Lic-chee   f   43   F   m   wife   yes   yes
175   John Philip   m   26   F   s   stp-son   yes   yes
176   (Ko-hi-lee)   m   21   F   s   son   yes   yes
177   Suc-tee   m   19   F   s   son   yes   yes
178   We-to-yee   f   17   F   s   dau   yes   yes
179   Git-ma-tee   f   13   F   s   dau   yes   yes

180   Johnny   m   32   F   m   Head   yes   yes
181   Eula   f   28   F   m   wife   yes   yes
182   Juanita   f   7   F   s   dau   yes   yes

183   Romeo   m   24   F   m   Head   yes   yes
184   Little   f   19   F   m   wife   yes   yes

FRANK

185   Miami   m   52   F   s   Head   yes   yes

FRAZIER

186   Bird   m   27   F   w   Head   yes   yes
187   Unknown   m   5   F   s   son   yes   yes
188   Unknown   m   2   F   s   son   yes   yes

61

Florida Seminoles Indian Census (As of April 1, 1932)

KEY: Census Number; Name; Sex; Age at Last Birthday; Tribe (Seminole, unless otherwise stated); Degree of Blood; Marital Status; Relationship to Head of Family; At Jurisdiction where enrolled [Yes or No] (If no, Where); Ward [Yes or No]; Allotment, Annuity, and Identification Numbers (if given).

GOPHER

189   Jim m 62 F w Head yes yes
190   **Tiger, Mary** f 72 F w sister yes yes
191   **Tiger, Ada** f 33 F s niece yes yes
192   **Tiger, Betty Mac** f 11 ¼ s grt-niece yes yes
193   **Tiger, Howard** m 7 ¼ s grt-nephew yes yes

194   Lucy f 49 F w Head yes yes
195   Sar-a-chee m 27 F s son yes yes
196   San-to-sah-yee f 21 F s dau yes yes
197   Ho-po-yo-yee f 19 F s dau yes yes
198   Carlisle Jim m 16 F s son yes yes
199   Unknown f 2 F s grnd-dau yes yes

HENRY

200   Jim m 41 F m Head yes yes
201   Tim-ac-kee f 32 F m wife yes yes
202   Unknown f 11 F s dau yes yes
203   Unknown m 8 F s son yes yes

HUFF

204   Sam m 49 F w Head yes yes
205   Pocahontas f 23 F s dau yes yes
206   George m 4 F s grnd-son yes yes

207   Frank m 19 F m Head yes yes
208   Ruby f 15 F m wife yes yes

JIM

209   Frank m 31 F s Head yes yes

210   Lazy m 36 F m Head yes yes
211   Mon-ta-kee f 30 F m wife yes yes

Florida Seminoles Indian Census (As of April 1, 1932)

KEY: Census Number; Name; Sex; Age at Last Birthday; Tribe (Seminole, unless otherwise stated); Degree of Blood; Marital Status; Relationship to Head of Family; At Jurisdiction where enrolled [Yes or No] (If no, Where); Ward [Yes or No]; Allotment, Annuity, and Identification Numbers (if given).

212	Unknown f 14 F s dau yes yes
213	Unknown f 13 F s dau yes yes
214	Ah-po-kee f 19 F s niece yes yes

| 215 | Jose m 37 F s Head yes yes |
| 216 | Unknown f 38 F s sis yes yes |

217	Webb m 35 F m Head yes yes
218	Unknown f 30 F m wife yes yes
219	Unknown m 13 F s son yes yes
220	Unknown m 11 F s son yes yes
221	Unknown f 9 F s dau yes yes
222	Unknown f 6 F s dau yes yes

223	Willie #1 m 42 F m Head yes yes
224	Unknown f 39 F m wife yes yes
225	Unknown f 12 F s dau yes yes
226	Unknown f 9 F s dau yes yes
227	Unknown f 7 F s dau yes yes

228	Willie #2 m 34 F m Head yes yes
229	Hick-chi-he-chlee f 21 F m wife yes yes
230	Unknown f 4 F s dau yes yes
231	Unknown f 2 F s dau yes yes

JIMMIE

232	Little m 32 F m Head yes yes
233	Unknown f 30 F m wife yes yes
234	Unknown f 14 F s dau yes yes
235	Unknown m 12 F s son yes yes

JOHNNY

236	Kir-kee m 37 F s Head yes yes
237	Sar-pi-kul-ker f 40 F s sister yes yes
238	Ma-har f 39 F s sister yes yes

Florida Seminoles Indian Census (As of April 1, 1932)

KEY: Census Number; Name; Sex; Age at Last Birthday; Tribe (Seminole, unless otherwise stated); Degree of Blood; Marital Status; Relationship to Head of Family; At Jurisdiction where enrolled [Yes or No] (If no, Where); Ward [Yes or No]; Allotment, Annuity, and Identification Numbers (if given).

JOHNS

239   Ernie   f   44   F   s   Head   yes   yes

240   Annie   f   66   F   w   Head   yes   yes
241   Fik-heth-lee   f   34   F   s   dau   yes   yes
242   Oscar   m   30   F   s   son   yes   yes
243   Fick-hi-chlee   f   28   F   s   dau   yes   yes
244   Pa-pa-kee   f   26   F   s   dau   yes   yes
245   Mok-har-po-che   f   24   F   s   dau   yes   yes
246   Sac-chee-wah   m   21   F   s   son   yes   yes
247   Ka-see-ha-chee   f   20   F   s   dau   yes   yes
248   Ar-nah   f   18   F   s   dau   yes   yes
249   In-kar-pak-kee   m   16   F   s   son   yes   yes
250   Lizzie   f   13   F   s   dau   yes   yes
251   Unknown   f   11   F   s   dau   yes   yes
252   Unknown   f   2   F   s   dau   yes   yes
253   **Gopher, Ada**   f   32   F   s   niece   yes   yes

JONES

254   Sam   m   38   F   m   Head   yes   yes
255   Missie Stick   f   36   F   m   wife   yes
256   Free   f   18   F   s   dau   yes   yes
257   Henry   m   15   F   s   son   yes   yes
258   Willie   m   12   F   s   son   yes   yes
259   Unknown   f   10   F   s   dau   yes   yes
260   Unknown   f   8   F   s   dau   yes   yes
261   Unknown   f   6   F   s   dau   yes   yes
262   Unknown   f   4   F   s   dau   yes   yes
263   Unknown   m   3   F   s   son   yes   yes
264   Sam   m   82   F   w   cousin   yes   yes

JOSH

265   John   m   23   ¼   s   Head   yes   yes

Florida Seminoles Indian Census (As of April 1, 1932)

KEY: Census Number; Name; Sex; Age at Last Birthday; Tribe (Seminole, unless otherwise stated); Degree of Blood; Marital Status; Relationship to Head of Family; At Jurisdiction where enrolled [Yes or No] (If no, Where); Ward [Yes or No]; Allotment, Annuity, and Identification Numbers (if given).

JUMPER

266	Mrs. Squirrel	f	52	F	w	Head	yes	yes
267	Stem-i-he-ooh	f	31	F	s	dau	yes	yes
268	Unknown	m	29	F	s	son	yes	yes
269	Charlie	m	67	F	m	Head	yes	yes
270	Wa-to-kee	f	59	F	m	wife	yes	yes
271	Boy	m	30	F	s	son	yes	yes
272	Buffalo Bill	m	27	F	s	son	yes	yes
273	Charlie Knight	m	23	F	m	Head	yes	yes
274	*(Illegible)*	f	?	F	m	wife	yes	yes
275	Unknown	m	5/12	F	s	stp-son	yes	yes
276	[Johnny] Cooter	m	45	F	m	Head	yes	yes
277	Unknown	f	52	F	m	wife	yes	yes
278	Unknown	m	39	F	s	stp-son	yes	yes
279	Miami Charlie	m	30	F	s	son	yes	yes
280	Unknown	f	25	F	s	dau	yes	yes
281	Unknown	f	23	F	s	dau	yes	yes
282	John Joy	m	27	F	s	Head	yes	yes
283	Fi-gi	f	57	F	w	mother	yes	yes
284	Jose	m	27	F	m	Head	yes	yes
285	Katie	f	26	F	m	wife	yes	yes
286	Moses	m	5	F	s	son	yes	yes
287	*(Illegible)*	f	?/12	F		dau	yes	yes
288	Little Charlie	m	50	F	m	Head	yes	yes
289	Sally	f	41	F	m	wife	yes	yes
290	Unknown	m	21	F	s	son	yes	yes
291	Unknown	f	18	F	s	dau	yes	yes
292	Holly	m	16	F	s	son	yes	yes
293	Ruby	f	14	F	s	dau	yes	yes
294	Unknown	f	10	F	s	dau	yes	yes

KEY: Census Number; Name; Sex; Age at Last Birthday; Tribe (Seminole, unless otherwise stated); Degree of Blood; Marital Status; Relationship to Head of Family; At Jurisdiction where enrolled [Yes or No] (If no, Where); Ward [Yes or No]; Allotment, Annuity, and Identification Numbers (if given).

295   Willie   m   62   F   s   Head   yes   yes

McKINLEY

296   William   m   37   F   m   Head   yes   yes
297   To-wee   f   30   F   m   wife   yes   yes
298   Homer   m   15   F   s   son   yes   yes
299   Mitty   f   13   F   s   dau   yes   yes
300   Dixie   m   11   F   s   son   yes   yes
301   Douglas   m   8   F   s   son   yes   yes
302   Unknown   m   5   F   s   son   yes   yes
303   Unknown   m   1   F   s   son   yes   yes

MICCO

304   Charlie   m   40   F   m   Head   yes   yes
305   Was-wah-kee   f   32   F   m   wife   yes   yes
306   Sa-ke-lat-kee   f   17   F   s   dau   yes   yes
307   Unknown   f   15   F   s   dau   yes   yes
308   Unknown   f   13   F   s   dau   yes   yes
309   Unknown   f   11   F   s   dau   yes   yes
310   To-tho-po-ho-chee   m   8   F   s   son   yes   yes
311   Little Jack   m   3   F   s   son   yes   yes

312   Oscar   m   35   F   m   Head   yes   yes
313   To-chee   f   32   F   m   wife   yes   yes
314   Unknown   f   14   F   s   dau   yes   yes
315   Unknown   f   11   F   s   dau   yes   yes
316   Unknown   f   10   F   s   dau   yes   yes
317   Unknown   f   8   F   s   dau   yes   yes
318   Unknown   m   6   F   s   son   yes   yes

MORGAN

319   Ely   m   38   F   s   Head   yes   yes
320   Unknown   f   72   F   w   mother   yes   yes
321   Jake   m   36   F   s   brother   yes   yes

KEY: Census Number; Name; Sex; Age at Last Birthday; Tribe (Seminole, unless otherwise stated); Degree of Blood; Marital Status; Relationship to Head of Family; At Jurisdiction where enrolled [Yes or No] (If no, Where); Ward [Yes or No]; Allotment, Annuity, and Identification Numbers (if given).

322	Ma-ma	f	27	F	s	sister	yes	yes	
323	**Milliard, Sheela Johns**	f	33	F	w	sister	yes	yes	

MOTLOE

324	Jack	m	38	F	m	Head	yes	yes
325	Belle	f	36	F	m	wife	yes	yes
326	Ollie	f	5	F	s	stp-dau	yes	yes
327	Unknown	f	3/12	F	s	dau	yes	yes

328	John	m	32	F	m	Head	yes	yes
329	Lon-he	f	19	F	m	wife	yes	yes
330	Jennie	f	47	F	w	cousin	yes	yes
331	Billie	m	77	F	w	father	yes	yes

OSCEOLA

332	Billie	m	40	F	m	Head	yes	yes
333	Ruby	f	36	F	m	wife	yes	yes
334	Tak-hat-a-see	f	21	F	s	dau	yes	yes
335	Unknown	f	18	F	s	dau	yes	yes
336	Che-ho-kee	m	16	F	s	son	yes	yes
337	Unknown	f	14	F	s	dau	yes	yes
338	Unknown	m	12	F	s	son	yes	yes
339	Unknown	m	10	F	s	son	yes	yes
340	Jimmie	m	8	F	s	son	yes	yes

341	Billy	m	41	F	w	Head	yes	yes
342	Unknown	f	14	F	s	dau	yes	yes
343	Unknown	f	12	F	s	dau	yes	yes
344	Unknown	m	10	F	s	son	yes	yes

345	Charlie	m	25	F	m	Head	yes	yes
346	Tommie Hand	f	33	F	m	wife	yes	yes
347	Unknown	m	5	F	s	son	yes	yes
348	Unknown	f	4	F	s	dau	yes	yes

Florida Seminoles Indian Census (As of April 1, 1932)

KEY: Census Number; Name; Sex; Age at Last Birthday; Tribe (Seminole, unless otherwise stated); Degree of Blood; Marital Status; Relationship to Head of Family; At Jurisdiction where enrolled [Yes or No] (If no, Where); Ward [Yes or No]; Allotment, Annuity, and Identification Numbers (if given).

349	Cori	m	27	F	m	Head	yes	yes	
350	Juanita	f	23	F	m	wife	yes	yes	
351	Unknown	f	3	F	s	dau	yes	yes	
352	Unknown	m	1	F	s	son	yes	yes	
353	George	m	52	F	m	Head	yes	yes	
354	Non-for-me	f	41	F	m	wife	yes	yes	
355	Ba-sof-tee	m	18	F	s	son	yes	yes	
356	William Buck	m	13	F	s	son	yes	yes
357	Unknown	f	12	F	s	dau	yes	yes	
358	Jim-Joy	m	38	F	m	Head	yes	yes	
359	Unknown	f	35	F	m	wife	yes	yes	
360	Unknown	f	19	F	s	dau	yes	yes	
361	Unknown	f	17	F	s	dau	yes	yes	
362	Unknown	m	13	F	s	son	yes	yes	
363	Jimmie	m	84	F	w	Head	yes	yes	
364	Mary	f	17	F	s	dau	yes	yes	
365	Stuman	m	15	F	s	son	yes		
366	Unknown	m	13	F	s	son	yes	yes	
367	John	m	61	F	m	Head	yes	yes	
368	Chaw-see	f	52	F	m	wife	yes	yes	
369	Unknown	f	20	F	s	dau	yes	yes	
370	Loc-kee	m	15	F	s	son	yes	yes	
371	Wah-tee	f	13	F	s	dau	yes	yes	
372	Unknown	f	8	F	s	dau	yes	yes	
373	John #2	m	50	F	m	Head	yes	yes	
374	Unknown	f	50	F	m	wife	yes	yes	
375	Unknown	f	27	F	s	dau	yes	yes	
376	Unknown	f	24	F	s	dau	yes	yes	
377	Unknown	f	22	F	s	dau	yes	yes	
378	Pal-i-kee	m	15	F	s	son	yes	yes	
379	[Richard] Yo-ho-lo-chee	m	27	F	m	Head	yes	yes

Florida Seminoles Indian Census (As of April 1, 1932)

KEY: Census Number; Name; Sex; Age at Last Birthday; Tribe (Seminole, unless otherwise stated); Degree of Blood; Marital Status; Relationship to Head of Family; At Jurisdiction where enrolled [Yes or No] (If no, Where); Ward [Yes or No]; Allotment, Annuity, and Identification Numbers (if given).

380   Lona f 17 F m wife yes yes

381   Robert m 20 F m Head yes yes
382   Unknown f 20 F m wife yes yes
383   Roy Nash m 1 F s son yes yes

384   Wit-kee f 40 F w Head yes yes
385   Unknown f 23 F s dau yes yes

PARKER

386   Argyl m 31 F s Head yes
387   Amelia f 36 F s sister yes yes

388   Courtney m 3? F w yes yes

389   Dan m 38 F m Head yes yes
390   Unknown f 33 F m wife yes yes
391   Unknown f 11 F s stp-dau yes yes
392   Unknown m 10 F s stp-son yes yes

PEACOCK

393   Charlie m 37 F s Head yes yes

PLATT

394   Josh m 28 ¼ s Head yes yes
395   Fi-kee f 70 ¼ w mother yes yes

PRETTY

396   Old f 64 F w Head yes yes

ROBERTS

397   Kar-nac-tee f 24 F s Head yes yes

69

KEY: Census Number; Name; Sex; Age at Last Birthday; Tribe (Seminole, unless otherwise stated); Degree of Blood; Marital Status; Relationship to Head of Family; At Jurisdiction where enrolled [Yes or No] (If no, Where); Ward [Yes or No]; Allotment, Annuity, and Identification Numbers (if given).

398	To-pi-kee	f	22	F	s	sister	yes	yes
399	Nat-cho-kee	m	16	F	s	brother	yes	yes
400	Lak-kee	m	13	F	s	brother	yes	yes

SMITH

401	Billie	m	82	F	m	Head	yes	yes
402	Mut-to-lo-kee	f	77	F	m	wife	yes	yes
403	Dolly	f	49	F	s	dau	yes	yes
404	Dick	m	51	F	m	Head	yes	yes
405	Hon-kee	f	47	F	m	wife	yes	yes
406	George	m	16	F	s	son	yes	yes
407	Lobie	f	15	F	s	dau	yes	yes
408	Wa-chee	m	10	F	s	son	yes	yes

409	Morgan	m	32	F	m	Head	yes	yes
410	Unknown	f	27	F	m	wife	yes	yes
411	Unknown	f	2	F	s	dau	yes	yes
412	Unknown	f	1	F	s	dau	yes	yes

413	Tom	m	43	F	m	Head	yes	yes
414	Stella	f	32	F	m	wife	yes	yes
415	Unknown	f	5	F	s	dau	yes	yes
416	Unknown	f	3	F	s	dau	yes	yes
417	Cully	f	34	F	s	sister	yes	yes

SNOW

418	Samson	m	36	F	m	Head	yes	yes
419	Co-pic-cha-ho-lee	f	31	F	m	wife	yes	yes
420	Unknown	m	9	F	s	son	yes	
421	Chat-lah-nok-kee	f	3	F	s	dau	yes	yes
422	Unknown	m	1	F	s	son	yes	yes

STEWART

423	Billie	m	57	F	m	Head	yes	yes

Florida Seminoles Indian Census (As of April 1, 1932)

KEY: Census Number; Name; Sex; Age at Last Birthday; Tribe (Seminole, unless otherwise stated); Degree of Blood; Marital Status; Relationship to Head of Family; At Jurisdiction where enrolled [Yes or No] (If no, Where); Ward [Yes or No]; Allotment, Annuity, and Identification Numbers (if given).

424	Susie	f	53	F	m	wife	yes	yes	
425	Fannie	f	30	F	s	dau	yes	yes	
426	Am-a-chee	f	92	F	w	mother	yes	yes	
427	Mar-po-hat-chee	f	25	F	s	niece	yes	yes	
428	**Charlie Big**	m	49	F	s	bro-in-law	yes	yes	
429	**Snow, Charlie**	m	36	F	s	nephew	yes	yes	
430	**Wells, Ben**	m	23	F	s	nephew	yes	yes	

TIGER

431	Brown	m	42	F	w	Head	yes	yes
432	Charlie	m	50	F	w	Head	yes	yes
433	Cuffney	m	54	F	m	Head	yes	yes
434	Unknown	f	51	F	m	wife	yes	yes
435	Doctor	m	53	F	w	Head	yes	yes
436	Emma	f	41	F	w	Head	yes	yes
437	Unknown	f	22	F	s	dau	yes	yes
438	Unknown	m	20	F	s	son	yes	yes
439	Frank	m	41	F	w	Head	yes	yes
440	Unknown	f	19	F	s	dau	yes	yes
441	Unknown	f	16	F	s	dau	yes	yes
442	Unknown	f	15	F	s	dau	yes	yes
443	Unknown	m	13	F	s	son	yes	yes
444	John Frank	m	21	F	m	Head	yes	yes
445	Lona	f	17	F	m	wife	yes	yes
446	Jim	m	50	F	m	Head	yes	
447	Unknown	f	60	F	m	wife	yes	yes
448	Little	m	29	F	s	son	yes	yes
449	Unknown	f	27	F	s	dau	yes	yes
450	Unknown	m	24	F	s	son	yes	yes
451	Unknown	m	20	F	s	son	yes	yes

Florida Seminoles Indian Census (As of April 1, 1932)

KEY: Census Number; Name; Sex; Age at Last Birthday; Tribe (Seminole, unless otherwise stated); Degree of Blood; Marital Status; Relationship to Head of Family; At Jurisdiction where enrolled [Yes or No] (If no, Where); Ward [Yes or No]; Allotment, Annuity, and Identification Numbers (if given).

452   Mrs. Miami John f 46 F w Head yes yes
453   Little m 20 F s son yes yes
455   Willie m 62 F w bro-in-law yes yes
456   **Billie, Unknown** m 41 F s bro-in-law yes yes

457   Nac-o-tee m 39 F w Head yes yes
458   Unknown m 22 F s son yes yes
459   Unknown f 18 F s dau yes yes
460   Unknown m 16 F s son yes yes
461   Unknown f 14 F s dau yes yes

462   Na-ha m 46 F m Head yes yes
463   Lucy f 54 F m wife yes yes

464   San-tee m 30 F s Head yes yes

465   Tiger m 37 F m Head yes yes
466   Ruby f 34 F m wife yes yes
467   Tiger Boy m 17 F s son yes
468   Mar-stook-kee f 15 F s dau yes yes
469   Frank m 13 F s son yes yes
470   Josie m 11 F s son yes yes
471   Cypress m 9 F s son yes yes
472   Harjo m 7 F s son yes yes
473   Unknown f 5 F s dau yes yes
474   Unknown f 1 F s dau yes yes

TIGERTAIL

475   Charlie m 62 F w Head yes yes
476   Cat-ath-kee m 16 F s son yes yes

477   *(Illegible)* m 22 F m Head yes yes
478   Ha-na-wee f 19 F m wife yes yes
479   Unknown f 10/12 F s dau yes yes
480   Unknown f 26 F s half-sister yes yes
481   Edna f 18 F s sister yes yes

KEY: Census Number; Name; Sex; Age at Last Birthday; Tribe (Seminole, unless otherwise stated); Degree of Blood; Marital Status; Relationship to Head of Family; At Jurisdiction where enrolled [Yes or No] (If no, Where); Ward [Yes or No]; Allotment, Annuity, and Identification Numbers (if given).

482   Lena f 16 F s sister yes yes
483   Martha f 14 F s sister yes yes
484   Francis f 11 F s sister yes yes

TOMMIE

485   Anna f 76 F w Head yes yes
486   Annie May f 39 F s dau yes yes
487   Brownie m 33 F s son yes yes

488   Ben m 49 F m Head yes yes
489   Tudle f 37 F m wife yes yes
490   Mary f 10 F s dau yes yes
491   **Tiger, Missie** f 44 F s sister-in-law yes yes
492   **Parker, Mary** f 10 F s niece yes yes
493   **Parker, Agnes** f 8 F s niece yes yes

494   Cho-bee [Mrs. Charlie] f 53 F w Head yes yes

495   Frank m 36 F m Head yes yes
496   Ho-mi-pee [Sally] f 26 F m wife yes yes
497   Ca-tho-nee [Willie Micco] m 5 F s son yes yes
498   Es-tah-kah-yee m 2 F s son yes yes

499   Jack m 34 F m Head yes yes
500   Charlotte f 27 F m wife yes yes
501   La-po-tee-kee [Herbert Hoover] m 12 F s son yes yes
502   We-cho-ka [George] m 10 F s son yes yes
503   Be-fa-tjo-kee [Fred Smith] m 8 s son yes yes
504   Fee-low-to-lee [Rosa Lee] f 7 F s dau yes yes
505   My-ta-lo-skee [O-Din] m 5 F s son yes yes
506   Why-ho-see [Edward] m 3 F s son yes yes

507   Cha-ma-lee-cha [Dick] m 1 F s son yes yes

508   Jim m 36 F m Head yes yes
509   Lo-bee f 28 F m wife yes yes

KEY: Census Number; Name; Sex; Age at Last Birthday; Tribe (Seminole, unless otherwise stated); Degree of Blood; Marital Status; Relationship to Head of Family; At Jurisdiction where enrolled [Yes or No] (If no, Where); Ward [Yes or No]; Allotment, Annuity, and Identification Numbers (if given).

510 Unknown m 5 F s son yes yes
511 **Bowers, Mrs. Jackson** f 2? F s yes yes
512 **Bowers, Unknown** m 2 F s nephew yes yes
513 Lody f 28 F s Head yes yes
514 Morgan Baby f 7 F s dau yes yes

515 To-pa-kee [Sam] m 27 F m Head yes yes
516 Mary f 18 F m wife yes yes
517 A-ta-let-kee [Jimmie] m 1 F s son yes yes

518 Small-pox m 45 F m Head yes yes
519 Mary f 37 F m wife yes yes

TONY

520 Young m 50 F m Head yes yes
521 Unknown f 44 F m wife yes yes
522 Sim-pa-ha-hee f 19 F s dau yes yes
523 Cla-sa-he-yee f 13 F s dau yes yes
524 **Billie, Jimmie** m 32 F s nephew yes yes
525 **Billie, Unknown** m 30 F s nephew yes yes
526 **Doctor, Jimmie** m 25 F s nephew yes yes
527 **Doctor, Unknown** f 27 F s niece yes yes

TUCKER

528 Chaw-huc-kee f 70 F w Head yes yes
529 Ho-po-thut-kee f 54 F s dau yes yes
530 Mait-kah f 51 F s dau yes yes
531 Sar-thler-nah-kee f 28 F s dau yes yes
532 Frank m 26 F s son yes yes
533 Nok-me-lee-kee m 26 F s grnd-son yes yes
534 Te-heth-lee-kee f 25 F s grnd-dau yes yes

535 Oscar m 36 F m Head yes yes
536 Cot-ner f 33 F m wife yes yes
537 Cus-sum-lak-chee f 17 F s dau yes yes

KEY: Census Number; Name; Sex; Age at Last Birthday; Tribe (Seminole, unless otherwise stated); Degree of Blood; Marital Status; Relationship to Head of Family; At Jurisdiction where enrolled [Yes or No] (If no, Where); Ward [Yes or No]; Allotment, Annuity, and Identification Numbers (if given).

538	Unknown m 14 F s son yes yes
539	Unknown m 11 F s son yes yes
540	Unknown m 8 F s son yes yes

WALKER

541	Henry m 64 F m Head yes yes
542	Unknown f 52 F m wife yes yes
543	Unknown f 28 F s dau yes yes

| 544 | Wat-cha-kee m 30 F s Head yes yes |

WILLIE

545	Frank m 47 F m Head yes yes
546	Ba-shec f 25 F m wife yes yes
547	O-mas-kee m 15 F s son yes yes
548	Yo-pote-ama f 13 F s dau yes yes

549	Jessie m 32 F m Head yes yes
550	Unknown f 29 F m wife yes yes
551	Unknown f 12 F s dau yes yes
552	Unknown f 11 F s dau yes yes

| 553 | Johnny m 62 F w Head yes yes |

554	Sam m 40 F m Head yes yes
555	Unknown f 32 F m wife yes yes
556	Henry m 13 F s son yes yes
557	Walter Roy m 10 F s son yes yes
558	Mary f 7 F s dau yes yes
559	Unknown m 5 F s son yes yes
560	**Charlie, Corinne** f 26 F w sister-in-law yes yes
561	**Charlie, Pauline** f 6 F s niece yes yes

KEY: Census Number; Name; Sex; Age at Last Birthday; Tribe (Seminole, unless otherwise stated); Degree of Blood; Marital Status; Relationship to Head of Family; At Jurisdiction where enrolled [Yes or No] (If no, Where); Ward [Yes or No]; Allotment, Annuity, and Identification Numbers (if given).

WILSON

562   Ben   m   28   F   s   Head   yes   yes
563   Unknown   f   17   F   s   sister   yes   yes

DEATHS
[For the Year 1932]

Billie, Ingram's child   f   5   F   s   9-1931

Billie, John's baby   f   1½   F   s   1-3-1932

Clay, Henry   m   58   F   m   9-15-1931

Dixie, Edwin   m   24   ¼   s   7-11-1931

Doctor, Grover   m   41   F   m   3-20-1932

Gopher, Son-fun-chee [John]   m   24   F   s   8-9-1931

Gopher, Willie   m   22   F   s   8-3-1931

Johns, Willie   m   60   F   m   12-6-1931

Tiger, John   m   54   F   m   1-1-1932

Tommie, Frank's baby [Rose Marie]   f   5/12   F   s   4-23-1938

Florida Seminoles Indian Census (As of April 1, 1932)

KEY: Census Number; Name; Sex; Age at Last Birthday; Tribe (Seminole, unless otherwise stated); Degree of Blood; Marital Status; Relationship to Head of Family; At Jurisdiction where enrolled [Yes or No] (If no, Where); Ward [Yes or No]; Allotment, Annuity, and Identification Numbers (if given).

DROPPED
(Died during previous years)

Buck, John's wife   f   ?   F   m   *(No date given)*
Jim, Miami   m   89   F   m   Died 3 yrs back

Tommie, Tony   m   31   F   s   4-1931

Tommie, Charlie   m   8 or 58   F   s   Died 2 yrs back

Tommie, Charlie   m   57   F   m   Died 2 yrs back

Florida Seminoles Indian Census (As of April 1, 1933)

KEY: Census Number Name Sex Age at Last Birthday Tribe (Seminole, unless otherwise stated) Degree of Blood Marital Status Relationship to Head of Family At Jurisdiction where enrolled [Yes or No] (If no, Where) Ward [Yes or No] Allotment, Annuity, and Identification Numbers (if given).

BILLIE

1	Sac-a-to-yee [Mrs. Carney]	f	33	F	w	Head	yes	yes
2	Lo-lee [Johnson]	m	14	F	s	son	yes	yes
3	He-chee [Johnny]	m	12	F	s	son	yes	yes
4	Edna [Ko-ta-kee]	f	10	F	s	dau	yes	yes
5	Larry	m	8	F	s	son	yes	yes
6	Minnie	f	6	F	s	dau	yes	yes
7	Peggy	f	2	F	s	dau	yes	yes
8	Unknown	f	?	F	s	dau	yes	yes
9	Charlie	m	52	F	m	Head	yes	yes
10	Mona	f	49	F	m	wife	yes	yes
11	Chestnut	m	27	F	s	son	yes	yes
12	Ruby	f	25	F	s	dau	yes	yes
13	Maggie	f	21	F	s	dau	yes	yes
14	Cowboy	m	23	F	m	Head	yes	yes
15	Annie	f	20	F	m	wife	yes	yes
16	Girtman	m	37	F	w	Head	yes	yes
17	Sa-wat-skee	m	15	F	s	son	yes	yes
18	Kunzie	m	37	F	m	Head	yes	yes
19	Addie	f	34	F	m	wife	yes	yes
20	Unknown	m	11	F	s	son	yes	yes
21	Unknown	f	3	F	s	dau	yes	yes
22	Little Charlie	m	36	F	m	Head	yes	yes
23	Chi-ki-kee	f	51	F	m	wife	yes	yes
24	Mary	f	36	F	w	Head	yes	yes
25	Willie #1	m	66	F	w	Head	yes	yes
26	John	m	27	F	m	Head	yes	yes
27	Ma-wee-ne-lee	f	39	F	m	wife	yes	yes
28	Homer	m	4	F	s	son	yes	yes

Florida Seminoles Indian Census (As of April 1, 1933)

KEY: Census Number Name Sex Age at Last Birthday Tribe (Seminole, unless otherwise stated) Degree of Blood Marital Status Relationship to Head of Family At Jurisdiction where enrolled [Yes or No] (If no, Where) Ward [Yes or No] Allotment, Annuity, and Identification Numbers (if given).

29 Unknown m 2 F s son yes yes

30 Willie #2 m 44 F w Head yes yes
31 Johnny m 19 F s son yes yes
32 George m 15 F s son yes yes

33 Yarber m 26 F m Head yes yes
34 Unknown f 21 F m wife yes yes
35 Unknown m 5 F s son yes yes

36 Grover m 37 F m Head yes yes
37 Unknown f 27 F m wife yes yes
38 Unknown m 16 F s son yes yes
39 Unknown f 14 F s dau yes yes

40 Ingram m 38 F m Head yes yes
41 Tak-ho-kee f 37 F m wife yes yes
42 Johnson m 19 F s son yes yes
43 Unknown m 17 F s son yes yes
44 Unknown m 14 F s son yes yes

45 John #2 m 88 F m Head yes yes
46 Hah-won-a-ha-yee f 20 F m wife yes yes
47 Effie f 8 F s dau yes yes
48 Unknown f 6 F s dau yes yes

49 Josie m 47 F m Head yes yes
50 Wat-see f 43 F m wife yes yes
51 E-sa-wee f 15 F s dau yes yes
52 Es-sta-yee f 10 F s dau yes yes
53 Li-to-e-kee f 7 F s dau yes yes
54 Sha-he-thee m 6 F s son yes yes

55 Robert m 32 F m Head yes yes
56 Josie f 33 F m wife yes yes
57 Milton m 3 F s son yes yes

58 Wilson m 31 F m Head yes yes

KEY: Census Number Name Sex Age at Last Birthday Tribe (Seminole, unless otherwise stated) Degree of Blood Marital Status Relationship to Head of Family At Jurisdiction where enrolled [Yes or No] (If no, Where) Ward [Yes or No] Allotment, Annuity, and Identification Numbers (if given).

59   Rosalee f 19 F m wife yes yes

BOWLEGS

60   Billy m 66 ¼ w Head yes yes
61   **Tucker, Lewis** m 48 ¼ s bro yes yes
62   **Pearce, Lucy** f 51 F w sis yes yes
63   **Pearce, Ada** f 22 F s niece yes yes
64   **Pearce, Anna** f 20 F s niece yes yes

BOWERS

65   Joe m 53 F m Head yes yes
66   Lena f 33 F m wife yes yes
67   Jackson m 24 F w son yes yes
68   Lydee f 21 F s dau yes yes
69   Dick m 17 F s son yes yes
70   Ka-pik-cha-ha-cho m 15 F s son yes yes
71   Unknown m 13 F s son yes yes
72   Unknown m 11 F s son yes yes
73   Unknown m 9 F s son yes yes

74   Lillie f 37 F w Head yes yes
75   Tom Buster m 14 F s son yes yes
76   Bessie Buster f 8 F s dau yes yes
77   **Willie, Ruby** f 42 F w sister yes yes
78   **Willie, Little** f 4 F s niece yes yes

BUCK

79   John m 35 F w Head yes yes

BUSTER

80   Billie m 66 F m Head yes yes
81   Nellie f 82 F m wife yes yes
82   Ar-nah f 64 F s stp-dau yes yes
83   Yek-am-kah f 34 F s dau yes yes

Florida Seminoles Indian Census (As of April 1, 1933)

KEY: Census Number Name Sex Age at Last Birthday Tribe (Seminole, unless otherwise stated) Degree of Blood Marital Status Relationship to Head of Family At Jurisdiction where enrolled [Yes or No] (If no, Where) Ward [Yes or No] Allotment, Annuity, and Identification Numbers (if given).

84   No-ket-wher f 34 F s dau yes yes

85   Charlie m 61 F w Head yes yes

86   Po-lah-lee f 53 F w Head yes yes
87   Addie f 34 F m dau yes yes
88   Little f 30 F s dau yes yes
89   Unknown f 26 F s dau yes yes

90   Johnny m 36 F s Head yes yes

91   Johnny m 43 F m Head yes yes
92   In-git-tah-yee f 45 F m wife yes yes
93   So-wah-ho-yee f 15 F s dau yes yes
94   Unknown m 5 F s son yes yes
95   Unknown m 4 F s son yes yes

CHARLIE

96   Chief m 26 F m Head yes yes
97   Rosalee f 36 F m wife yes yes
98   **Huff, Suc-leet-kee [Alice]** F 17 F s stp- dau yes yes
99   **Huff, Unknown** f 10/12 F s dau yes yes [Mother - Alice Huff]

100   Frank m 22 F m Head yes yes
101   Ko-hi-lee [Carrie] f 21 F m wife yes yes

CLAY

102   Ka-ki-kee f 43 F w Head yes yes
103   Abraham Lincoln m 35 F s son yes yes
104   Jack Johnson m 29 F s son yes yes
105   To-li-kee f 27 F s dau yes yes
106   Ta-la-kee f 21 F s dau yes yes
107   Nac-ho-mee f 13 F s dau yes yes

Florida Seminoles Indian Census (As of April 1, 1933)

KEY: Census Number Name Sex Age at Last Birthday Tribe (Seminole, unless otherwise stated) Degree of Blood Marital Status Relationship to Head of Family At Jurisdiction where enrolled [Yes or No] (If no, Where) Ward [Yes or No] Allotment, Annuity, and Identification Numbers (if given).

CYPRESS

108	Charlie m 58 F m Head yes yes
109	Lee f 49 F m wife yes yes
110	Henry m 19 F s son yes yes
111	To-ma-fino f 7 F s dau yes yes
112	Stanley Hanson m 5 F s son yes yes

| 113 | Futch m 63 F m Head yes yes |
| 114 | Unknown f 46 F m wife yes yes |

| 115 | Henry m 28 F m Head yes yes |
| 116 | To-ho-kee f 17 F m wife yes yes |

117	Johnny m 31 F m Head yes yes
118	My-ho-chee f 29 F m wife yes yes
119	Unknown m 11 F s son yes yes
120	Unknown m 5 F s son yes yes
121	Little m 27 F m Head yes yes
122	Unknown m 21 F m wife yes yes
123	Unknown m 2/12 (5-6-1933) F s son yes yes

124	Whitney m 53 F m Head yes yes
125	Sally f 41 F m wife yes yes
126	Suc-la-to-kee f 19 F s dau yes yes
127	See-ho-kee f 17 F s dau yes yes
128	Look-eet-see m 14 F s son yes yes
129	Che-na-see f 11 F s dau yes yes
130	Unknown m 10 F s son yes yes

131	Wilson m 45 F m Head yes yes
132	Ruby f 35 F m wife yes yes
133	Unknown f 17 F s dau yes yes
134	Unknown f 16 F s dau yes yes
135	Unknown f 15 F s dau yes yes
136	Unknown m 10 F s son yes yes

KEY: Census Number Name Sex Age at Last Birthday Tribe (Seminole, unless otherwise stated) Degree of Blood Marital Status Relationship to Head of Family At Jurisdiction where enrolled [Yes or No] (If no, Where) Ward [Yes or No] Allotment, Annuity, and Identification Numbers (if given).

DIXIE

137 Charlie m 61 ¼ m Head yes yes
138 Jim-sling f 56 F m wife yes yes
139 Walter Huff m 28 ¼ s son yes yes
140 Susie f 23 ¼ s dau yes yes
141 Samson m 11 ¼ s son yes yes
142 **Billy, Mrs. Miami** f 98 F w mother-in-law yes yes

DOCTOR

143 Cologne m 37 F m Head yes yes
144 Unknown f 32 F m wife yes yes
145 Unknown m 17 F s son yes yes
146 Unknown m 13 F s son yes yes
147 Unknown m 10 F s son yes yes
148 Unknown f 3 F s dau yes yes

149 Nac-o-tee [Mrs. Grover] f 34 F w Head yes yes
150 Unknown m 11 F s son yes yes
151 Unknown f 10 F s dau yes yes
152 Unknown f 3 F s dau yes yes

153 Hal m 38 F m Head yes yes
154 Annie f 38 F m wife yes yes
155 Lat-i-kee m 15 F s son yes yes
156 Unknown m 13 F s son yes yes
157 Unknown f 11 F s dau yes yes
158 Co-cop-cho-tee m 9 F s son yes yes
159 She-cho-pee m 7 F s son yes yes

160 Unknown f 52 F w Head yes yes
161 Unknown m 14 F s son yes yes
162 Unknown m 12 F s son yes yes
163 Unknown f 10 F s dau yes yes

164 Little m 65 f m Head yes yes
165 Mamie f 37 F m wife yes yes

KEY: Census Number Name Sex Age at Last Birthday Tribe (Seminole, unless otherwise stated) Degree of Blood Marital Status Relationship to Head of Family At Jurisdiction where enrolled [Yes or No] (If no, Where) Ward [Yes or No] Allotment, Annuity, and Identification Numbers (if given).

166 Tommie m 13 F s son yes yes

167 Wilson m 33 F m Head yes yes
168 O-cha-fish-shee f 34 F m wife yes yes
169 Unknown m 4 F s son yes yes

DRUITT

170 Jimmy m 33 F m Head yes yes
171 Unknown f 21 F m wife yes yes
172 Unknown f 11 F s dau yes yes
173 Unknown m 9 F s son yes yes
174 Unknown m 5 F s son yes yes

FEWELL

175 Charlie m 57 F m Head yes yes
176 Lic-chee f 44 F m wife yes yes
177 John Philip m 27 F s stp-son yes yes
178 Unknown m 22 F s son yes yes
179 Suc-tee m 20 F s son yes yes
180 We-to-yee f 18 F s dau yes yes
181 Git-ma-tee f 14 F s dau yes yes

182 Johnny m 32 F m Head yes yes
183 Eula f 29 F m wife yes yes
184 Juanita f 8 F s dau yes yes
185 Romeo m 25 F m Head yes yes
186 Little f 20 F m wife yes yes

FRANK

187 Miami m 53 F s Head yes yes

FRAZIER

188 Bird m 28 F w Head yes yes
189 Unknown m 6 F s son yes yes

KEY: Census Number Name Sex Age at Last Birthday Tribe (Seminole, unless otherwise stated) Degree of Blood Marital Status Relationship to Head of Family At Jurisdiction where enrolled [Yes or No] (If no, Where) Ward [Yes or No] Allotment, Annuity, and Identification Numbers (if given).

190   Unknown m 3 F s son yes yes

GOPHER

191   Jim m 63 F w Head yes yes
192   **Tiger, Mary** f 73 F w sister yes yes
193   **Tiger, Ada** f 34 F s niece yes yes
194   **Tiger, Betty Mae** f 14 ¼ s grnd-niece yes yes
195   **Tiger, Howard** m 9 ¼ f grnd-nephew yes yes

196   Lucy f 50 F w Head yes yes
197   Sar-a-chee m 28 F s son yes yes
198   San-to-sah-yee f 22 F s dau yes yes
199   Ho-po-ye-yee f 20 F s dau yes yes
200   Carlisle Jim m 17 F s son yes yes
201   Unknown f 3 F s grnd-dau yes yes

HENRY

202   Jim m 43 F m Head yes yes
203   Tim-ak-kee f 33 F m wife yes yes
204   Unknown f 12 F s dau yes yes
205   Unknown m 10 F s son yes yes

HUFF

206   Sam m 50 F w Head yes yes
207   Pocahontas f 24 F s dau yes yes
208   George m 5 F s grnd-son yes yes
209   Frank m 20 F w son yes yes

210   Ruby f 16 F w Head yes yes [Willie Bille's dau]
                                                  [Separated from Frank Huff]

JIM

211   Frank m 32 F s Head yes yes
212   Lazy m 36 F m Head yes yes

Florida Seminoles Indian Census (As of April 1, 1933)

KEY: Census Number Name Sex Age at Last Birthday Tribe (Seminole, unless otherwise stated) Degree of Blood Marital Status Relationship to Head of Family At Jurisdiction where enrolled [Yes or No] (If no, Where) Ward [Yes or No] Allotment, Annuity, and Identification Numbers (if given).

213   Mon-ta-kee f 31 F m wife yes yes
214   Unknown f 15 F s dau yes yes
215   Unknown f 14 F s dau yes yes
216   Ah-po-kee f 20 F s niece yes yes

217   Josie m 38 F s Head yes yes
218   Unknown f 39 F s sister yes yes

219   Webb m 36 F m Head yes yes
220   Unknown f 31 F m wife yes yes
221   Unknown m 14 F s son yes yes
222   Unknown m 12 F s son yes yes
223   Unknown f 10 F s dau yes yes
224   Unknown f 7 F s dau yes yes

225   Willie #1 m 43 F m Head yes yes
226   Unknown m 40 m wife yes yes
227   Unknown f 13 F s dau yes yes
228   Unknown f 10 f s dau yes yes

229   Willie #2 m 35 F m Head yes yes
230   Hick-chi-he-chlee f 22 F m wife yes yes
231   Unknown f 5 F s dau yes yes
232   Unknown f 3 F s dau yes yes

JIMMIE

233   Little m 33 F m Head yes yes
234   Unknown f 31 f m wife yes yes
235   Unknown f 15 F s dau yes yes
236   Unknown m 13 f s son yes yes

JOHNNY

237   Kir-kee m 38 f s Head yes yes
238   Sar-pi-kul-ker f 41 F s sister yes yes
239   Ma-har f 40 f s sister yes yes

Florida Seminoles Indian Census (As of April 1, 1933)

KEY: Census Number Name Sex Age at Last Birthday Tribe (Seminole, unless otherwise stated) Degree of Blood Marital Status Relationship to Head of Family At Jurisdiction where enrolled [Yes or No] (If no, Where) Ward [Yes or No] Allotment, Annuity, and Identification Numbers (if given).

JOHNS

240	Annie	f	67	F	w	Head	yes	yes	
241	Fik-heth-lee [Dolly]	f	35	F	s	dau	yes	yes	
242	Sa-mok-ka [Oscar]	m	31	F	s	son	yes	yes	
243	Fik-hi-chlee [Ada]	f	29	F	s	dau	yes	yes	
244	Pa-po-kee [Arnie]	f	27	F	s	dau	yes	yes	
245	Ho-see-ha-cha [Lizzie]	f	25	F	s	dau	yes	yes	
246	Sak-cha-wee [Tobie]	m	23	F	s	son	yes	yes	
247	Ka-see-ha-chee	f	21	F	s	dau	yes	yes	
248	Mit-to-ta-kee [Barfield]	m	19	F	s	son	yes	yes	
249	Is-ting-kop-ta [Lillie]	f	17	F	s	dau	yes	yes	
250	Mamia	f	14	F	s	dau	yes	yes	
251	Unknown	f	11	F	s	dau	yes	yes	
252	Unknown	f	3	¼	s	grnd-dau	yes	yes	
253	Lucy	f	5/12 (11-30-1932)	¼	s	grnd-dau	yes	yes	
254	**Gopher, Ada**	f	34	F	s	niece	yes	yes	
255	Ernie	f	45	F	s	Head	yes	yes	

JONES

256	Sam	m	39	F	m	Head	yes	yes	
257	Missie Stick	f	37	F	m	wife	yes	yes	
258	Free	f	19	F	s	dau	yes	yes	
259	Henry	m	16	F	s	son	yes	yes	
260	Willie	m	13	F	s	son	yes	yes	
261	Unknown	f	11	F	s	dau	yes	yes	
262	Unknown	f	9	F	s	dau	yes	yes	
263	Unknown	f	7	F	s	dau	yes	yes	
264	Unknown	f	5	F	s	dau	yes	yes	
265	Unknown	m	4	F	s	son	yes	yes	
266	Unknown	m	11/12 (5-1-1932)	F	s	son	yes	yes	
267	Sam, Sr	m	83	F	w	cousin	yes	yes	

JOSH

268	John	m	23	¼	s	Head	yes	yes	

Florida Seminoles Indian Census (As of April 1, 1933)

KEY: Census Number Name Sex Age at Last Birthday Tribe (Seminole, unless otherwise stated) Degree of Blood Marital Status Relationship to Head of Family At Jurisdiction where enrolled [Yes or No] (If no, Where) Ward [Yes or No] Allotment, Annuity, and Identification Numbers (if given).

<u>JUMPER</u>

269	Charlie	m	68	F	m	Head	yes	yes
270	Wa-to-kee	f	61	F	m	wife	yes	yes
271	Boy	m	31	f	s	son	yes	yes
272	Buffalo Bill	m	28	F	s	son	yes	yes

273 Charlie Knight m 23 F m Head yes yes
274 Lena f 21 F m wife yes yes
275 Kat-ath-fee [Tom] m 1 F s son yes yes

276 Cooter [Johnny] m 46 F m Head yes yes
277 Unknown f 53 F m wife yes yes
278 Unknown m 41 F s stp-son yes yes
279 Miami Charlie m 31 F s son yes yes
280 Unknown f 26 F s dau yes yes
281 Unknown f 24 F s dau yes yes

282 Harry m 22 F m Head yes yes
283 Shen-ta-skahe-chee f 24 F m wife yes yes
284 Joe m 10/12 F s son yes yes

285 John Joy m 28 F s Head yes yes
286 Fi-gi f 58 F w mother yes yes

287 Josie m 28 F m Head yes yes
288 Katy f 27 f m wife yes yes
289 Moses m 6 F s son yes yes

290 Mus-lee-chee f 1 F s Head yes yes

291 Little Charlie m 51 F m Head yes yes
292 Sally f 42 F m wife yes yes
293 Unknown f 19 F s dau yes yes
294 Holly m 17 F s son yes yes
295 Ruby f 15 F s dau yes yes
296 Unknown f 11 F s dau yes yes

KEY: Census Number Name Sex Age at Last Birthday Tribe (Seminole, unless otherwise stated) Degree of Blood Marital Status Relationship to Head of Family At Jurisdiction where enrolled [Yes or No] (If no, Where) Ward [Yes or No] Allotment, Annuity, and Identification Numbers (if given).

297	Mrs. Squirrel	f	53	F	w	Head	yes	yes
298	Stem-i-he-ooh	f	33	f	s	dau	yes	yes
299	Unknown	m	30	F	s	son	yes	yes
300	Willie	m	63	F	s	Head	yes	yes

McKINLEY

301	William	m	38	F	m	Head	yes	yes
302	To-wee	f	31	F	m	wife	yes	yes
303	Homer	m	16	F	s	son	yes	yes
304	Mitty	f	14	F	s	dau	yes	yes
305	Dixie	m	12	F	s	son	yes	yes
306	Douglas	m	9	F	s	son	yes	yes
307	Unknown	m	6	F	s	son	yes	yes
308	Unknown	m	2	f	s	son	yes	yes

MICCO

309	Charlie	m	41	F	m	Head	yes	yes
310	Was-wah-kee	f	33	F	m	wife	yes	yes
311	Sa-ko-lat-kee	f	18	F	s	dau	yes	yes
312	Unknown	f	16	F	s	dau	yes	yes
313	Unknown	f	14	F	s	dau	yes	yes
314	Unknown	f	12	F	s	dau	yes	yes
315	Te-the-po-ho-chee	m	9	F	s	son	yes	yes
316	Little Jack	m	4	F	s	son	yes	yes
317	Oscar	m	36	F	m	Head	yes	yes
318	To-chee	f	33	F	m	wife	yes	yes
319	Unknown	f	15	F	s	dau	yes	yes
320	Unknown	f	13	F	s	dau	yes	yes
321	Unknown	f	11	f	s	dau	yes	yes
322	Unknown	f	9	F	s	dau	yes	yes
323	Unknown	m	7	F	s	son	yes	yes

Florida Seminoles Indian Census (As of April 1, 1933)

KEY: Census Number Name Sex Age at Last Birthday Tribe (Seminole, unless otherwise stated) Degree of Blood Marital Status Relationship to Head of Family At Jurisdiction where enrolled [Yes or No] (If no, Where) Ward [Yes or No] Allotment, Annuity, and Identification Numbers (if given).

MORGAN

324	Ely	m	39	F	s	Head	yes	yes	
325	Unknown	f	73	F	w	mother	yes	yes	
326	Jake	m	37	F	s	brother	yes	yes	
327	Ma-ma	f	28	F	s	sister	yes	yes	
328	Unknown	f	6/12	F	s	niece	yes	yes	
329	**Hillard, Sheela Johns**	f	35	F	w	sister	yes	yes	

MOTLOE

330	Jack	m	39	f	m	Head	yes	yes
331	Belle	f	37	F	m	wife	yes	yes
332	Ollie	f	6	F	s	dau	yes	yes
333	Unknown	f	1	F	s	dau	yes	yes
334	John	m	33	F	m	Head	yes	yes
335	Les-hee	f	20	f	m	wife	yes	yes
336	Jennie	f	48	F	w	cousin	yes	yes
337	Billie	m	78	F	w	father	yes	yes

OSCEOLA

338	Billie	m	41	F	m	Head	yes	yes
339	Ruby	f	37	F	m	wife	yes	yes
340	Tak-hat-a-see	f	22	F	s	dau	yes	yes
341	Unknown	f	19	F	s	dau	yes	yes
342	Che-ho-kee	m	17	F	s	son	yes	yes
343	Unknown	f	15	F	s	dau	yes	yes
344	Unknown	m	13	F	s	son	yes	yes
345	Unknown	m	11	F	s	son	yes	yes
346	Jimmie	m	9	F	s	son	yes	yes
347	Billie #2	m	42	F	w	Head	yes	yes
348	Unknown	f	15	F	s	dau	yes	yes
349	Unknown	f	13	F	s	dau	yes	yes
350	Unknown	m	11	F	s	son	yes	yes

Florida Seminoles Indian Census (As of April 1, 1933)

KEY: Census Number Name Sex Age at Last Birthday Tribe (Seminole, unless otherwise stated) Degree of Blood Marital Status Relationship to Head of Family At Jurisdiction where enrolled [Yes or No] (If no, Where) Ward [Yes or No] Allotment, Annuity, and Identification Numbers (if given).

351	Charlie m 26 F m Head yes yes
352	Tommie Hand f 34 F m wife yes yes
353	Unknown m 6 F s son yes yes
354	Unknown f 5 f s dau yes yes

355	Cori m 28 F m Head yes yes
356	Juanita f 24 F m wife yes yes
357	Unknown f 5 F s dau yes yes
358	Unknown m 2 f s son yes yes

359	George m 53 F m Head yes yes
360	Non-for-mee f 42 F m wife yes yes
361	Ba-sef-tee m 19 F s son yes yes
362	William Buck m 14 F s son yes yes
363	Unknown f 13 f s dau yes yes

364	Jim-Joy m 39 F m Head yes yes
365	Unknown f 36 F m wife yes yes
366	Unknown f 20 F s dau yes yes
367	Unknown f 18 f s dau yes yes
368	Unknown m 15 F s son yes yes

369	Jimmie m 85 F w Head yes yes
370	Mary f 18 F s dau yes yes
371	Stuman m 16 f s son yes yes
372	Unknown m 14 f s son yes yes

373	John m 62 F m Head yes yes
374	Chaw-see f 53 F m wife yes yes
375	Loc-kee m 16 F s son yes yes
376	Wah-tee f 14 F s dau yes yes
377	Unknown f 9 F s dau yes yes

378	John #2 m 51 F m Head yes yes
379	Unknown f 51 F m wife yes yes
380	Unknown f 28 F s dau yes yes
381	Unknown f 25 F s dau yes yes
382	Unknown f 23 F s dau yes yes

Florida Seminoles Indian Census (As of April 1, 1933)

KEY: Census Number Name Sex Age at Last Birthday Tribe (Seminole, unless otherwise stated) Degree of Blood Marital Status Relationship to Head of Family At Jurisdiction where enrolled [Yes or No] (If no, Where) Ward [Yes or No] Allotment, Annuity, and Identification Numbers (if given).

383   Pal-i-kee m 16 F s son yes yes

384   Ye-ho-le-chee [Richard] m 28 F m Head yes yes
385   Lena f 18 F m wife yes yes
386   Unknown f 1/12 F s dau yes yes

387   Robert m 21 F m Head yes yes
388   Unknown f 21 F m wife yes yes
389   Roy Nash m 2 f s son yes yes
390   Unknown f 1/12 F s dau yes yes

391   Wit-kee f 41 F w Head yes yes
392   Unknown f 24 F s dau yes yes

PARKER

393   Argyl m 32 F s Head yes yes
394   Amelia f 37 F s sister yes yes

395   Courtney f 39 F w Head yes yes
396   Unknown f 6/12 F s dau yes yes

397   Dan m 39 F m Head yes yes
398   Unknown f 34 F m wife yes yes
399   **Jim, Unknown** f 12 F s stp-dau yes yes
400   **Jim, Unknown** m 11 F s stp-son yes yes [Johnny Jim's children]

PEACOCK

401   Charlie m 38 F s Head yes yes

PLATT

402   Josh m 29 ¼ s Head yes yes
403   Fi-kee f 71 ¼ w mother yes yes

Florida Seminoles Indian Census (As of April 1, 1933)

KEY: Census Number Name Sex Age at Last Birthday Tribe (Seminole, unless otherwise stated) Degree of Blood Marital Status Relationship to Head of Family At Jurisdiction where enrolled [Yes or No] (If no, Where) Ward [Yes or No] Allotment, Annuity, and Identification Numbers (if given).

PRETTY

404 Old m 65 F w Head yes yes

ROBERTS

405 U-ak-chee [Elsie] f 23 F s Head yes yes
406 Nat-cho-kee m 17 F s brother yes yes
407 Lak-kee m 14 F s brother yes yes

SMITH

408 Billie m 83 F m Head yes yes
409 Mut-to-lo-kee f 78 F m wife yes yes
410 Dolly f 50 F s dau yes yes

411 Dick m 52 F m Head yes yes
412 Hop-kee f 48 F m wife yes yes
413 George m 17 F s son yes yes
414 Lobie f 16 F s dau yes yes
415 Wa-chee m 11 F s son yes yes

416 Morgan m 33 F m Head yes yes
417 Unknown f 28 F m wife yes yes
418 Unknown f 3 F s dau yes yes
419 Unknown f 2 F s dau yes yes
420 Unknown m 6/12 (10-18-1932) F s son yes yes

421 Tom m 44 F m Head yes yes
422 Stella f 33 F m wife yes yes
423 Unknown f 6 F s dau yes yes
424 Unknown m 4 F s son yes yes
425 Cully f 35 F s sister yes yes

SNOW

426 Samson m 37 F m Head yes yes
427 Co-pic-cha-ho-lee f 32 F m wife yes yes

KEY: Census Number Name Sex Age at Last Birthday Tribe (Seminole, unless otherwise stated) Degree of Blood Marital Status Relationship to Head of Family At Jurisdiction where enrolled [Yes or No] (If no, Where) Ward [Yes or No] Allotment, Annuity, and Identification Numbers (if given).

428   Unknown m 9 F s son yes yes
429   Chat-lah-nok-kee f 4 F s dau yes yes
430   Unknown m 2 f s son yes yes

STEWART

431   Billie m 58 F m Head yes yes
432   Susie f 54 F m wife yes yes
433   Fannie f 31 F s dau yes yes
434   Am-a-chee f 93 F w mother yes yes
435   Mar-po-hat-chee f 26 F s niece yes yes
436   **Charlie, Big** m 50 F s brother-in-law yes yes
437   **Snow, Charlie** m 37 F s nephew yes yes
438   **Wells, Ben** m 24 F s nephew yes yes

TIGER

439   Brown m 43 F w Head yes yes

440   Charlie m 51 F w Head yes yes

441   Cuffney m 55 F m Head yes yes
442   Unknown f 52 F m wife yes yes

443   Doctor m 54 F w Head yes yes

444   Emma f 42 F w Head yes yes
445   Unknown f 23 F s dau yes yes
446   Unknown m 21 F s son yes yes

447   Frank m 42 F w Head yes yes
448   Unknown f 20 F s dau yes yes
449   Unknown f 18 F s dau yes yes
450   Unknown f 16 F s dau yes yes
451   Unknown m 14 F s son yes yes

452   John Frank m 22 F m Head yes yes
453   Lena f 18 F m wife yes yes

Florida Seminoles Indian Census (As of April 1, 1933)

KEY: Census Number Name Sex Age at Last Birthday Tribe (Seminole, unless otherwise stated) Degree of Blood Marital Status Relationship to Head of Family At Jurisdiction where enrolled [Yes or No] (If no, Where) Ward [Yes or No] Allotment, Annuity, and Identification Numbers (if given).

454   Jim m 51 F m Head yes yes
455   Unknown f 61 F m wife yes yes
456   Little m 30 F s son yes yes
457   Unknown f 28 F s dau yes yes
458   Unknown m 25 F s son yes yes
459   Unknown m 21 F s son yes yes

460   Mrs. Miami John f 47 F w Head yes yes
461   Willie m 63 F w bro-in-law yes yes
462   **Billie, Home Spun** m 42 F s bro-in-law yes yes

463   Nac-o-tee m 40 F w Head yes yes
464   Unknown m 23 F s son yes yes
465   Unknown f 19 f s dau yes yes
466   Unknown m 17 F s son yes yes
467   Unknown f 15 F s dau yes yes

468   Na-ha m 47 F m Head yes yes
469   Lucy f 55 F m wife yes yes

470   San-tee m 31 F s Head yes yes

471   Tiger m 38 F m Head yes yes
472   Ruby f 35 F m wife yes yes
473   Tiger Boy m 18 F s son yes yes
474   Mar-stook-kee f 16 F s dau yes yes
475   Frank m 14 F s son yes yes
476   Josie m 12 F s son yes yes
477   Cypress m 10 F s son yes yes
478   Harjo m 8 F s son yes yes
479   Unknown f 6 F s dau yes yes
480   Unknown f 2 F s dau yes yes

TIGERTAIL

481   Charlie m 63 F w Head yes yes
482   Kat-ath-lee m 17 F s son yes yes

95

KEY: Census Number Name Sex Age at Last Birthday Tribe (Seminole, unless otherwise stated) Degree of Blood Marital Status Relationship to Head of Family At Jurisdiction where enrolled [Yes or No] (If no, Where) Ward [Yes or No] Allotment, Annuity, and Identification Numbers (if given).

483   Wilson m 23 F m Head yes yes
484   Ha-ha-wee f 20 F m wife yes yes
485   Unknown f 2 F s dau yes yes
486   Unknown f 26 F s half-sis yes yes
487   Edna f 19 F s sis yes yes
488   Lena f 17 F s sis yes yes
489   Martha f 15 F s sis yes yes
490   Francis f 12 F s sis yes yes

TOMMIE

491   Anna f 77 F w Head yes yes
492   Annie Mae f 40 F s dau yes yes
493   Brownie m 34 F s son yes yes

494   Ben m 50 F m Head yes yes
495   Tudie f 38 F m wife yes yes
496   Mary f 11 F s dau yes yes
497   **Tiger, Missie** f 45 F s sis-in-law yes yes
498   **Parker, Mary** f 11 F s niece yes yes
499   **Parker, Agnes** f 9 F s niece yes yes

500   Cho-bee [Mrs. Charlie] f 54 F w Head yes yes

501   Frank m 37 F m Head yes yes
502   Ho-mi-pee [Sadie] f 27 F m wife yes yes
503   Ka-tho-nee [Willie Micco] m 6 F s son yes yes
504   O-kay Es-tah-kah-yee m 3 F s son yes yes

505   Jack m 35 F m Head yes yes
506   Charlotte f 28 F m wife yes yes
507   La-po-too-kee [Herbert Hoover] m 13 F s son yes yes
508   Wo-cho-ka [George] m 11 F s son yes yes
509   Be-fa-tho-kee [Fred Smith] m 9 F s son yes yes
510   Fee-lo-to-kee [Rosa Lee] f 8 F s dau yes yes
511   My-ta-lo-skee [Odin] m 6 F s son yes yes
512   Why-he-sca [Edward] m 4 F s son yes yes
513   Cha-ma-lee-cha [Dick] m 2 f s son yes yes

Florida Seminoles Indian Census (As of April 1, 1933)

KEY: Census Number Name Sex Age at Last Birthday Tribe (Seminole, unless otherwise stated) Degree of Blood Marital Status Relationship to Head of Family At Jurisdiction where enrolled [Yes or No] (If no, Where) Ward [Yes or No] Allotment, Annuity, and Identification Numbers (if given).

514 Jim m 37 F m Head yes yes
515 Lo-bee f 29 F m wife yes yes
516 Unknown m 6 F s son yes yes

517 Lady f 29 F ? Head yes yes
518 Baby Morgan f 8 F (s) dau yes yes

519 Te-pa-kee [Sam] m 28 F m Head yes yes
520 Se-hen-ne-thee [Mary] f 19 F m wife yes yes
521 A-ta-let-kee [Jimmie] m 2 F s son yes yes
522 Unknown f 6/12 F s dau yes yes

523 Small-pox m 46 F m Head yes yes
524 Mary f 38 F m wife yes yes

TONY

525 Young m 51 F m Head yes yes
526 Unknown f 45 F m wife yes yes
527 Sim-pa-ha-hee f 20 F s dau yes yes
528 Cla-sa-he-yee f 14 F s dau yes yes
529 **Billie, Jimmie** m 33 F s nephew yes yes
530 **Billie, Unknown** m 31 F s nephew yes yes
531 **Doctor, Jimmie** m 26 F s nephew yes yes
532 **Doctor, Unknown** f 28 F s niece yes yes

TUCKER

533 Chaw-huc-kee f 71 F w Head yes yes
534 Ho-po-thut-kee f 55 F s dau yes yes
535 Mait-kah f 52 F s dau yes yes
536 Sar-thler-na-kee f 29 F s dau yes
537 Frank m 27 F s son yes yes
538 Nok-me-lee-kee m 27 F s grnd-son yes yes
539 Te-heth-lee-kee f 25 F s grnd-son yes yes
540 Oscar m 37 F m Head yes yes
541 Cot-net f 34 F m wife yes yes
542 Cox-sum-lak-chee f 18 F s dau yes yes

KEY: Census Number Name Sex Age at Last Birthday Tribe (Seminole, unless otherwise stated) Degree of Blood Marital Status Relationship to Head of Family At Jurisdiction where enrolled [Yes or No] (If no, Where) Ward [Yes or No] Allotment, Annuity, and Identification Numbers (if given).

543	Unknown	m	15	F	s	son	yes	yes	
544	Unknown	m	12	F	s	son	yes	yes	
545	Unknown	m	9	F	s	son	yes	yes	

WALKER

546	Henry	m	65	F	m	Head	yes	yes
547	Unknown	f	53	F	m	wife	yes	yes
548	Unknown	f	29	F	s	dau	yes	yes
549	Wat-cha-kee	m	31	f	s	Head	yes	yes

WILLIE

550	Frank	m	48	F	m	Head	yes	yes
551	Ba-shee	f	26	F	m	wife	yes	yes
552	O-mas-kee	m	16	F	s	son	yes	yes
553	Yo-pote-ema	f	14	F	s	dau	yes	yes
554	Jessie	m	33	F	m	Head	yes	yes
555	Unknown	f	30	F	m	wife	yes	yes
556	Unknown	f	13	F	s	dau	yes	yes
557	Unknown	f	12	F	s	dau	yes	yes
558	Johnny	m	63	F	w	Head	yes	yes
559	Sam	m	41	F	m	Head	yes	yes
560	Unknown	f	33	F	m	wife	yes	yes
561	Henry	m	14	F	s	son	yes	yes
562	Walter Roy	m	11	f	s	son	yes	yes
563	Mary	f	8	F	s	dau	yes	yes
564	Unknown	m	5	F	s	son	yes	yes
565	**Charlie, Corinne**	f	27	F	w	sis-in-law	yes	yes
566	**Charlie, Pauline**	f	7	F	s	niece	yes	yes

WILSON

567	Ben	m	29	F	s	Head	yes	yes

KEY: Census Number Name Sex Age at Last Birthday Tribe (Seminole, unless otherwise stated) Degree of Blood Marital Status Relationship to Head of Family At Jurisdiction where enrolled [Yes or No] (If no, Where) Ward [Yes or No] Allotment, Annuity, and Identification Numbers (if given).

568   Unknown f 18 F s sister yes yes

DEATHS
(For 1933)

44   Billie, Edna f 11 F s Died 4-25-1933   [Ingram Billie's child]

120   Cypress, Unknown f 10/12 F s Died 5-1932 [Johnny Cypress' girl]

128   Fewell, Billie m 94 F w Died 7-17-1933

227   Jim, Unknown f 7 F s Died 12-26-1932 [Willie Jim's girl]

453   Tiger, Little m 20 F s Died 12-26-1932 [Mrs. Miami John Tiger's son]

        Buster, Unknown m / F s Still birth [Johnny Buster's child]

        Willie, Unknown f 6 da F s Died 4-6-1933   [Frank Willie's baby]

DROPPED
(Duplications)

74   Bowers, Mrs. Jackson f 29 [Lillie Bowers]

78   Bowers, Unknown m 3 [Little Willie]

Florida Seminoles Indian Census (As of April 1, 1934)

KEY: Census Number Name Sex Age at Last Birthday Tribe (Seminole, unless otherwise stated) Degree of Blood Marital Status Relationship to Head of Family At Jurisdiction where enrolled [Yes or No] (If no, Where) Ward [Yes or No] Allotment, Annuity, and Identification Numbers (if given).

BILLIE

1	Albert m 34 F m Head yes yes
2	Willie f 30 F m wife yes yes
3	Unknown f 4 F s dau yes yes
4	Unknown f 10/12 F s dau yes yes
5	Charlie m 53 F m Head yes yes
6	Mona f 50 F m wife yes yes
7	Chestnut m 28 F s son yes yes
8	Ruby f 26 F s dau yes yes
9	Maggie f 22 F s dau yes yes
10	Cowboy m 24 F w Head yes yes
11	Frank m 18 F m Head yes yes
12	Ruby f 16 F m wife yes yes
13	Ingram m 39 F m Head yes yes
14	Tak-ho-kee f 38 F m wife yes yes
15	Unknown f 7 F s dau yes yes
16	Charlie m 18 F w son yes yes
17	Jimmie #1 m 20 F m Head yes yes
18	Cla-sa-he-ye Tony f 15 F m wife yes yes
19	Unknown m ½[sic] F s son yes yes
20	Jimmie #2 m 34 F m Head yes yes
21	Unknown f 29 F m wife yes yes
22	John #1 m 28 F m Head yes yes
23	Ma-wee-he-lee f 40 F m wife yes yes
24	Homer m 5 F s son yes yes
25	Unknown m 1 F s son yes yes
26	John #2 m 89 F w Head yes yes
27	Josie m 48 F m Head yes yes

Florida Seminoles Indian Census (As of April 1, 1934)

KEY: Census Number Name Sex Age at Last Birthday Tribe (Seminole, unless otherwise stated) Degree of Blood Marital Status Relationship to Head of Family At Jurisdiction where enrolled [Yes or No] (If no, Where) Ward [Yes or No] Allotment, Annuity, and Identification Numbers (if given).

28   Wat-see f 44 F m wife yes yes
29   Camilla f 16 F s dau yes yes
30   Effie f 11 F s dau yes yes
31   Frances f 8 F s dau yes yes
32   Paul m 7 F s son yes yes

33   Kunzie m 38 F m Head yes yes
34   Addie f 35 F m wife yes yes
35   Unknown f 12 F s dau yes yes
36   Unknown m 2 F s son yes yes

37   Little Charlie m 37 F m Head yes yes
38   Chi-ki-kee f 52 F m wife yes yes

39   Mary f 37 F w Head yes yes

40   Romeo m 26 F m Head yes yes
41   Little f 21 F m wife yes yes
42   Unknown m 2 F s son yes yes

43   Robert m 33 F m Head yes yes
44   Josie f 34 F m wife yes yes
45   Milton m 4 f s son yes yes
46   Weaver m 2 F s son yes yes
47   **Morgan, Jess** m 19 F s nephew yes yes
48   **Buster, Billie** m 27 F s brother yes yes
49   Sa-wat-skee m 16 F s nephew yes yes

50   Rosalie f 20 F w Head yes yes
51   Edna [Ko-ta-kee] f 16 F s niece yes yes
52   Johnson [Lo-lee] m 14 F s nephew yes yes
53   Johnny [He-chee] m 12 F s nephew yes yes
54   Minnie [Wit-kee] f 10 F s niece yes yes
55   Larry m 9 F s nephew yes yes
56   Unknown f 7 F s niece yes yes
57   Peggy f 3 F s niece yes yes

58   Willie #1 m 57 F m Head yes yes

Florida Seminoles Indian Census (As of April 1, 1934)

KEY: Census Number Name Sex Age at Last Birthday Tribe (Seminole, unless otherwise stated) Degree of Blood Marital Status Relationship to Head of Family At Jurisdiction where enrolled [Yes or No] (If no, Where) Ward [Yes or No] Allotment, Annuity, and Identification Numbers (if given).

59	Hah-won-a-ha-yee f 21 F m wife yes yes
60	Effie f 9 F s stp-dau yes yes
61	Unknown f 7 F s stp-dau yes yes

62	Willie #2 m 45 F w Head yes yes
63	Johnny m 20 F s son yes yes
64	George m 16 F s son yes yes
65	Wilson m 32 F w Head yes yes
66	Yarber m 27 F m Head yes yes
67	Unknown f 22 F m wife yes yes
68	Unknown m 6 F s son yes yes
69	Unknown f 3 F s dau yes yes

BOWERS

70	Joe m 54 F m Head yes yes
71	Lena f 34 F m wife yes yes
72	Andrew Jackson m 25 F w son yes yes
73	Lydee f 22 F s dau yes yes
74	Dick m 18 F s son yes yes
75	Ka-pik-cha-ha-cho m 16 F s son yes yes
76	Unknown m 14 F s son yes yes
77	Unknown m 12 F s son yes yes
78	Unknown m 10 F s son yes yes

79	Lillie f 38 F w Head yes yes
80	Tom Buster m 15 F s son yes yes
81	Bessie Buster f 9 F s dau yes yes
82	Shah-pali-ki-lee f 3 F s dau yes yes
83	**Willie, Ruby** f 43 F w sis yes yes
84	**Willie, Little** f 5 F s niece yes yes

BOWLEGS

85	Billy m 67 ½ w Head yes yes
86	**Tucker, Lewis** m 49 ½ s bro yes yes
87	**Pearce, Lucy** f 52 F w sis yes yes
88	**Pearce, Ada** f 23 F s niece yes yes

Florida Seminoles Indian Census (As of April 1, 1934)

89   **Pearce, Anna** f 21 F s niece yes yes

BUCK

90   John m 36 F w Head yes yes

BUSTER

91   Billie m 67 F w Head yes yes
92   Mrs. Billie [Nellie] f 83 F w Head yes yes
93   Annie f 65 F s dau yes yes
94   Yek-am-kah f 35 F s dau yes yes
95   No-ket-cher f 35 F s dau yes yes

96   Charlie m 62 F w Head yes yes

97   Johnny #1 m 37 F s Head yes yes

98   Johnny #2 m 44 F m Head yes yes
99   In-git-tah-yee f 46 F m wife yes yes
100   So-wah-ho-yee f 16 F s stp-dau yes yes
101   Unknown m 7 F s son yes yes
102   Unknown f 5 F s dau yes yes

103   Mis-tee f 54 F w Head yes yes
104   Lois f 27 F s dau yes yes

CHARLIE

105   Frank m 23 F m Head yes yes
106   Carrie f 22 F m wife yes yes

CLAY

107   Mrs. Henry f 44 F w Head yes yes
108   Abraham Lincoln m 36 F s son yes yes
109   Jack Johnson m 30 F s son yes yes
110   To-li-kee f 28 F s dau yes yes

KEY: Census Number Name Sex Age at Last Birthday Tribe (Seminole, unless otherwise stated) Degree of Blood Marital Status Relationship to Head of Family At Jurisdiction where enrolled [Yes or No] (If no, Where) Ward [Yes or No] Allotment, Annuity, and Identification Numbers (if given).

| 111 | Ta-la-kee f 22 F s dau yes yes |
| 112 | Nac-ho-mee f 14 F s dau yes yes |

CYPRESS

113	Charlie m 63 F m Head yes yes
114	Lee f 50 F m wife yes yes
115	To-ma-fino f 8 F s dau yes yes
116	Stanley Hanson m 6 F s son yes yes

117	Frank m 20 F m Head yes yes
118	Unknown f 18 F m wife yes yes
119	Unknown m 9/12 F s son yes yes
120	Futch m 58 F m Head yes yes
121	Unknown f 47 F m wife yes yes
122	Unknown m 10 F s son yes yes
123	Unknown m 8 f s son yes yes

124	Johnny m 32 F m Head yes yes
125	O-ko-see f 30 F m wife yes yes
126	Unknown m 7 F s son yes yes
127	Unknown m 6 F s son yes yes
128	Unknown f 10/12 F s dau yes yes

129	Henry m 29 F m Head yes yes
130	To-ho-kee f 18 F m wife yes yes
131	Mary f 1 F s dau yes yes

132	Little m 28 F m Head yes yes
133	Unknown f 22 f m wife yes yes
134	Unknown m 1 F s son yes yes

135	Whitney m 54 F m Head yes yes
136	Sally f 42 F m wife yes yes
137	Suc-la-ti-kee f 20 F s dau yes yes
138	Sec-ho-kee f 18 F s dau yes yes
139	Look-eet-see m 15 F s son yes yes
140	Che-na-see f 12 F s dau yes yes

Florida Seminoles Indian Census (As of April 1, 1934)

KEY: Census Number Name Sex Age at Last Birthday Tribe (Seminole, unless otherwise stated) Degree of Blood Marital Status Relationship to Head of Family At Jurisdiction where enrolled [Yes or No] (If no, Where) Ward [Yes or No] Allotment, Annuity, and Identification Numbers (if given).

141	Unknown m 11 F s son yes yes

141   Unknown m 11 F s son yes yes

142   Wilson m 46 F m Head yes yes
143   Ruby f 36 F m wife yes yes
144   Unknown f 18 F s dau yes yes
145   Unknown f 17 F s dau yes yes
146   Unknown f 16 F s dau yes yes
147   Unknown f 11 F s son yes yes

DIXIE

148   Charlie m 62 ½ m Head yes yes
149   Jim-sling f 57 F m wife yes yes
150   Walter Huff m 29 ¾ s son yes yes
151   Susie f 24 ¾ s dau yes yes
152   Samson m 12 ¾ s son yes yes
153   **Billy, Mrs. Miami** f 99 F w mother-in-law yes yes
154   Unknown m 9/12 7/8 s grnd-son yes yes

DOCTOR

155   Cologne m 38 F m Head yes yes
156   Unknown f 33 F m wife yes yes
157   Unknown m 18 F s son yes yes
158   Unknown m 14 F s son yes yes
159   Unknown m 11 F s son yes yes
160   Unknown f 4 F s dau yes yes

161   Little m 66 F m Head yes yes
162   Mamie f 38 F m wife yes yes
163   Tommie m 14 F s son yes yes

164   Unknown f 53 F w Head yes yes
165   Unknown m 15 F s son yes yes
166   Unknown m 13 F s son yes yes
167   Unknown f 11 F s dau yes yes

168   Wilson m 34 F m Head yes yes

KEY: Census Number Name Sex Age at Last Birthday Tribe (Seminole, unless otherwise stated) Degree of Blood Marital Status Relationship to Head of Family At Jurisdiction where enrolled [Yes or No] (If no, Where) Ward [Yes or No] Allotment, Annuity, and Identification Numbers (if given).

169	O-sha-fish-shee f 35 F m wife yes yes
170	Unknown m 5 F s son yes yes
171	Unknown m 10/12 F s son yes yes

FEWELL

172	Charlie m 58 F m Head yes yes
173	Lic-chee f 45 F m wife yes yes
174	John Philip m 28 F s stp-son yes yes
175	Suc-tee m 21 F s son yes yes
176	We-ti-yee f 19 F s dau yes yes
177	Git-ma-tee f 10 F s dau yes yes

178	Johnny m 33 F m Head yes yes
179	Eula f 30 F m wife yes yes
180	Juanita f 9 F s dau yes yes

FRANK

181 Miami m 54 F s Head yes yes

FRAZIER

182 Bird m 29 F w Head yes yes

GOPHER

183	Jim m 64 F w Head yes yes
184	**Tiger, Mary** f 74 F w sister yes yes
185	**Tiger, Ada** f 35 F s niece yes yes
186	**Tiger, Betty Mae** f 15 ½ s grnd-niece yes yes
187	**Tiger, Howard** m 10 ½ s grnd-nephew yes yes
188	Lucy Tiger f 51 F w Head yes yes
189	Willie m 21 F s son yes yes
190	Annie f 17 F s dau yes yes
191	Lena f 16 F s dau yes yes
192	John Henry m 18 F s son yes yes

Florida Seminoles Indian Census (As of April 1, 1934)

KEY: Census Number Name Sex Age at Last Birthday Tribe (Seminole, unless otherwise stated) Degree of Blood Marital Status Relationship to Head of Family At Jurisdiction where enrolled [Yes or No] (If no, Where) Ward [Yes or No] Allotment, Annuity, and Identification Numbers (if given).

HENRY

193   Jim m 44 F w Head yes yes

194   Mrs. Jim f 34 F w Head yes yes
195   Unknown f 13 F s dau yes yes
196   Unknown m 11 F s son yes yes

HUFF

197   Sam m 51 F w Head yes yes

198   Frank m 21 F m Head yes yes
199   Mary f 19 F m wife yes yes

JIM

200   Frank m 33 F m Head yes yes
201   Annie f 21 F m wife yes yes

202   Johnnie m 37 F m Head yes yes
203   Mon-ta-kee f 32 F m wife yes yes
204   Unknown f 12 f s dau yes yes
205   Unknown m 10 F s son yes yes
206   Ah-po-kee f 10 F s niece yes yes
207   Unknown m 16 F s nephew yes yes

208   Josie m 39 F s Head yes yes
209   Unknown f 49 F s sis yes yes

210   Willie #1 m 44 F m Head yes yes
211   Unknown f 41 F m wife yes yes
212   Unknown f 14 F s dau yes yes
213   Unknown f 11 F s dau yes yes

214   Willie #2 m 36 F m Head yes yes
215   Hick-chi-he-chlee f 23 F m wife yes yes
216   Unknown f 13 F s dau yes yes

KEY: Census Number Name Sex Age at Last Birthday Tribe (Seminole, unless otherwise stated) Degree of Blood Marital Status Relationship to Head of Family At Jurisdiction where enrolled [Yes or No] (If no, Where) Ward [Yes or No] Allotment, Annuity, and Identification Numbers (if given).

217 Unknown f 10 F s dau yes yes
218 Unknown f 8 F s dau yes yes
219 Unknown m ½ F s son yes yes

220 Willie #3 m 37 F m Head yes yes
221 Unknown f 32 F m wife yes yes
222 Unknown m 15 F s son yes yes
223 Unknown m 13 F s son yes yes
224 Unknown f 11 F s dau yes yes
225 Unknown f 8 F s dau yes yes
226 Unknown m 6 F s son yes yes
227 Unknown m 3 f s son yes yes

228 Wa-ti-kee f 62 F w Head yes yes
229 Boy m 32 F s son yes yes
230 Buffalo Bill m 29 F s son yes yes
231 Unknown f 15 F s dau yes yes

JIMMIE

232 Little m 34 F m Head yes yes
233 Unknown f 32 F m wife yes yes
234 Unknown f 16 F s dau yes yes
235 Unknown m 14 F s son yes yes

JOHNNY

236 Kir-kee m 39 F s Head yes yes
237 Sar-pi-kul-ker f 42 F s sister yes yes
238 Ma-har f 41 F s sister yes yes

JOHNS

239 Annie f 68 F w Head yes yes
240 Dolly f 36 F s dau yes yes
241 Oscar m 32 F s son yes yes
242 Ada f 30 F s dau yes yes
243 Arnie f 28 F s dau yes yes

KEY: Census Number Name Sex Age at Last Birthday Tribe (Seminole, unless otherwise stated) Degree of Blood Marital Status Relationship to Head of Family At Jurisdiction where enrolled [Yes or No] (If no, Where) Ward [Yes or No] Allotment, Annuity, and Identification Numbers (if given).

244	Lizzie	f	26	F	s	dau	yes	yes	
245	Tobie	m	24	F	s	son	yes	yes	
246	Ka-see-na-chee	f	22	F	s	dau	yes	yes	
247	Barfield	m	20	F	s	son	yes	yes	
248	Lillie	f	18	F	s	dau	yes	yes	
249	Mamie	f	15	F	s	dau	yes	yes	
250	Lena	f	13	F	s	dau	yes	yes	
251	Lottie	f	4 ½	s		grnd-dau	yes	yes	
252	Lucy	f	1 ½	s		grnd-dau	yes	yes	
253	Ada	f	35	F	s	niece	yes	yes	
254	Ernie	f	46	F	s	Head	yes	yes	
255	Sheela Hillard	f	36	F	w	Head	yes	yes	
256	Maud	f	16	F	s	dau	yes	yes	
257	Joe	m	13	f	s	son	yes	yes	

JONES

258	Sam	m	40	F	m	Head	yes	yes	
259	Missie Stick	f	38	F	m	wife	yes	yes	
260	Free	f	20	F	s	dau	yes	yes	
261	Henry	m	17	F	s	son	yes	yes	
262	Willie	m	14	F	s	son	yes	yes	
263	Unknown	f	12	F	s	dau	yes	yes	
264	Unknown	f	10	F	s	dau	yes	yes	
265	Unknown	f	8	F	s	dau	yes	yes	
266	Unknown	f	5	F	s	dau	yes	yes	
267	Unknown	m	5	F	s	son	yes	yes	
268	Unknown	m	1	F	s	son	yes	yes	

JOSH

269	John	m	24	¾	s	Head	yes	yes	
270	Fi-kee	f	72	½	w	mother	yes	yes	

Florida Seminoles Indian Census (As of April 1, 1934)

JUMPER

271   Chief Charlie m 27 F m Head yes yes
272   Rosaliee f 37 F m wife yes yes
273   **Huff, Alice** f 18 F s stp-dau yes yes
274   **Huff, Unknown** f 1 F s dau yes yes

275   Charlie Knight [John] m 24 F m Head yes yes
276   Lena Huff f 22 F m wife yes yes
277   Tom m 2 F s son yes yes
278   Mary f 8/12 F s dau yes yes

279   Harry m 23 F m Head yes yes
280   Shen-ta-shake-chee f 25 F m wife yes yes
281   Joe m 1 F s son yes yes

282   John Joy m 29 F s Head yes yes
283   Fi-gi f 59 F w mother yes yes

284   Johnny m 47 F m Head yes yes
285   Unknown f 54 F m wife yes yes
286   Unknown f 27 F s dau yes yes

287   Josie m 29 F m Head yes yes
288   Pocahontas f 25 F m wife yes yes
289   **Huff, George** m 6 F s stp-son yes yes

290   Katy f 28 F w Head yes yes
291   Moses m 7 F s son yes yes
292   Lura f 2 F s dau yes yes

293   Little Charlie m 52 F m Head yes yes
294   Sally f 43 F m wife yes yes
295   Ruby f 16 F s dau yes yes
296   Horace m 12 F s son yes yes

297   Mrs. Squirrel f 54 F w Head yes yes
298   Stem-i-he-ooh f 34 F s dau yes yes

KEY: Census Number Name Sex Age at Last Birthday Tribe (Seminole, unless otherwise stated) Degree of Blood Marital Status Relationship to Head of Family At Jurisdiction where enrolled [Yes or No] (If no, Where) Ward [Yes or No] Allotment, Annuity, and Identification Numbers (if given).

299 Unknown m 30 F s son yes yes
300 **Tigertail, Kat-ath-lee** m 18 F s friend yes yes

301 Willie m 64 F s Head yes yes

MICCO

302 Charlie m 42 F m Head yes yes
303 Was-wah-kee f 34 F m wife yes yes
304 Sa-ko-lat-kee f 19 F s dau yes yes
305 Unknown f 17 F s dau yes yes
306 Unknown f 15 F s dau yes yes
307 Unknown f 13 F s dau yes yes
308 Te-the-oi-ho-chee m 10 F s son yes yes
309 Little Jack m 5 F s son yes yes
310 Unknown m 9/12 F s son yes yes

311 Oscar m 37 F m Head yes yes
312 To-chee f 34 F m wife yes yes
313 Unknown f 16 F s dau yes yes
314 Unknown f 14 F s dau yes yes
315 Unknown f 12 F s dau yes yes
316 Unknown f 10 F s dau yes yes
317 Unknown m 8 F s son yes yes

MORGAN

318 Ely m 40 F s Head yes yes

319 Jake m 38 F m Head yes yes
320 Unknown f 29 F m wife yes yes
321 **Smith, Unknown** f 4 F s stp-dau yes yes
322 **Smith, Unknown** m 3 F s stp-son yes yes
323 **Smith, Unknown** m 1 F s stp-son yes yes
324 Ma-ma f 29 F s sister yes yes
325 Unknown f 1 F s niece yes yes

Florida Seminoles Indian Census (As of April 1, 1934)

KEY: Census Number Name Sex Age at Last Birthday Tribe (Seminole, unless otherwise stated) Degree of Blood Marital Status Relationship to Head of Family At Jurisdiction where enrolled [Yes or No] (If no, Where) Ward [Yes or No] Allotment, Annuity, and Identification Numbers (if given).

MOTLOE

326   Jack m 40 F m Head yes yes
327   Belle f 38 F m wife yes yes
328   Ollie f 7 F s stp-dau yes yes
329   Unknown f 2 F s dau yes yes

330   John m 34 F m Head yes yes
331   Les-hee f 21 F m wife yes yes
332   Jennie f 49 F w cousin yes yes
333   Billie m 78 F w father yes yes

OSCEOLA

334   Billie #1 m 42 F m Head yes yes
335   Ruby f 38 F m wife yes yes
336   Tak-hat-a-see f 23 F s dau yes yes
337   Unknown f 20 F s dau yes yes
338   Che-ho-kee m 18 F s son yes yes
339   Unknown f 16 F s dau yes yes
340   Unknown m 14 F s son yes yes
341   Unknown m 12 F s son yes yes
342   Jimmie m 10 F s son yes yes

343   Billie #2 m 43 F w Head yes yes
344   Unknown f 16 F s dau yes yes
345   Unknown f 14 F s dau yes yes
346   Unknown m 12 F s son yes yes
347   **Doctor, John** m 36 F w bro-in-law yes yes
348   **Doctor, Unknown** m 18 F s nephew yes yes
349   **Doctor, Unknown** f 9 F s niece yes yes

350   Charlie m 27 F m Head yes yes
351   Tommie Hand f 35 F m wife yes yes
352   Unknown m 7 F s son yes yes
353   Unknown f 6 F s dau yes yes

354   Cori m 29 F m Head yes yes

Florida Seminoles Indian Census (As of April 1, 1934)

KEY: Census Number Name Sex Age at Last Birthday Tribe (Seminole, unless otherwise stated) Degree of Blood Marital Status Relationship to Head of Family At Jurisdiction where enrolled [Yes or No] (If no, Where) Ward [Yes or No] Allotment, Annuity, and Identification Numbers (if given).

355	Juanita	f	25	F	m	wife	yes	yes		
356	Unknown	f	6	F	s	dau	yes	yes		
357	Unknown	m	3	F	s	son	yes	yes		
358	Unknown	m	1	F	s	son	yes	yes		
359	George	m	54	F	m	Head	yes	yes		
360	Non-for-mee	f	43	F	m	wife	yes	yes		
361	Ba-sef-tee	m	20	F	s	son	yes	yes		
362	William Buck	m	15	F	s	son	yes	yes		
363	Unknown	f	14	F	s	dau	yes	yes		
364	Jimmie	m	86	F	w	Head	yes	yes		
365	Harjo	m	18	f	s	son	yes	yes		
366	Robert	m	16	F	s	son	yes	yes		
367	Stuman	m	10	F	s	son	yes	yes		
368	Billy	m	8	F	s	son	yes	yes		
369	Jimmie Druitt	m	34	F	m	Head	yes	yes		
370	Unknown	f	34	F	m	wie	yes	yes		
371	Unknown	m	17	F	s	son	yes	yes		
372	Unknown	m	15	F	s	son	yes	yes		
373	Unknown	f	14	F	s	dau	yes	yes		
374	Unknown	m	10	F	s	son	yes	yes		
375	Unknown	m	4	F	s	son	yes	yes		
376	Unknown	m	7/12	F	s	son	yes	yes		
377	John #1	m	63	F	m	Head	yes	yes		
378	Chaw-see	f	54	F	m	wife	yes	yes		
379	Jack	m	17	F	s	son	yes	yes		
380	**Frazier, John Bird**	m	7	F	s	grnd-son	yes	yes		
381	**Frazier, Henry Bird**	m	4	F	s	grnd-son	yes	yes		
382	John #2	m	52	F	m	Head	yes	yes		
383	Unknown	f	52	F	m	wife	yes	yes		
384	Unknown	f	26	F	s	dau	yes	yes		
385	Unknown	f	24	F	s	dau	yes	yes		
386	Richard	m	28	F	w	Head	yes	yes		

Florida Seminoles Indian Census (As of April 1, 1934)

KEY: Census Number Name Sex Age at Last Birthday Tribe (Seminole, unless otherwise stated) Degree of Blood Marital Status Relationship to Head of Family At Jurisdiction where enrolled [Yes or No] (If no, Where) Ward [Yes or No] Allotment, Annuity, and Identification Numbers (if given).

387   Francis m 1 f s son yes yes

388   Robert m 22 F m Head yes yes
389   Unknown f 22 F m wife yes yes
390   Roy Nash m 3 F s son yes yes
391   Unknown f 1 F s dau yes yes

392   William McKinley m 39 F m Head yes yes
393   To-wee f 32 F m wife yes yes
394   Homer m 17 F s son yes yes
395   Mitty f 15 F s dau yes yes
396   Dixie m 13 F s son yes yes
397   Douglas m 10 F s son yes yes
398   Unknown m 7 F s son yes yes
399   Unknown m 6 F s son yes yes
400   Unknown m 3 F s son yes yes
401   Unknown f 2 f s dau yes yes

402   Wit-kee f 42 F w Head yes yes
403   Unknown f 25 F s dau yes yes
404   Unknown m 19 F s son yes yes

PARKER

405   Argyl m 35 F s Head yes yes
406   Amelia f 38 F s sister yes yes

407   Courtney f 40 F w Head yes yes
408   Unknown f 1 F s dau yes yes

409   Dan m 40 F m Head yes yes
410   Unknown f 35 f m wife yes yes
411   **Jim, Unknown** f 13 F s stp-dau yes yes
412   **Jim, Unknown** m 12 F s stp-son yes yes

PEACOCK

413   Charlie m 39 F s Head yes yes

Florida Seminoles Indian Census (As of April 1, 1934)

KEY: Census Number Name Sex Age at Last Birthday Tribe (Seminole, unless otherwise stated) Degree of Blood Marital Status Relationship to Head of Family At Jurisdiction where enrolled [Yes or No] (If no, Where) Ward [Yes or No] Allotment, Annuity, and Identification Numbers (if given).

PRETTY

414   Old m 66 F w Head yes yes

ROBERTS

415   Elsie f 17 F s Head yes yes
416   Billy m 15 F s bro yes yes

SMITH

417   Dick m 53 F m Head yes yes
418   Hon-kee f 49 F m wife yes yes
419   George m 18 F s son yes yes
420   Lobie f 17 F s dau yes yes
421   Wa-chee m 12 f s son yes yes

422   Morgan m 34 F w Head yes yes
423   Mrs. Billie f 79 F w mother yes yes
424   Dolly f 51 F s sister yes yes

425   Tom m 45 F m Head yes yes
426   Stella f 34 F m wife yes yes
427   Unknown f 7 F s dau yes yes
428   Unknown m 5 F s son yes yes
429   Cully f 36 F s sister yes yes

SNOW

430   Samson m 38 F m Head yes yes
431   Co-pic-cha-ho-lee f 33 F m wife yes yes
432   Unknown m 10 F s son yes yes
433   Chat-lah-nok-kee f 5 F s dau yes yes
434   Unknown f 3 F s dau yes yes

STEWART

435   Billie m 59 F m Head yes yes

Florida Seminoles Indian Census (As of April 1, 1934)

KEY: Census Number Name Sex Age at Last Birthday Tribe (Seminole, unless otherwise stated) Degree of Blood Marital Status Relationship to Head of Family At Jurisdiction where enrolled [Yes or No] (If no, Where) Ward [Yes or No] Allotment, Annuity, and Identification Numbers (if given).

436   Susie f 55 F m wife yes yes
437   Fannie f 32 F s dau yes yes
438   Mar-po-hat-chee f 27 F s niece yes yes
439   **Charlie, Big** m 51 F s bro-in-law yes yes
440   **Snow, Charlie** m 38 F s nephew yes yes
441   **Wells, Ben** m 25 F s nephew yes yes
442   **Wells, Unknown** f 19 F s niece yes yes

TIGER

443   Brown m 44 F w Head yes yes

444   Charlie m 52 F w Head yes yes

445   Cuffney m 56 F m Head yes yes
446   Unknown f 52 f m wife yes yes
447   Unknown f 10 F m stp-dau yes yes
448   Doctor m 55 F w Head yes yes

449   Im-ho-kee Emma f 43 F w Head yes yes
450   Poland Poole f 24 F s dau yes yes
451   John Poole m 22 F s son yes yes

452   Frank m 43 F m Head yes yes
453   Nac-o-tee f 35 F m wife yes yes
454   Unknown f 21 F s dau yes yes
455   Unknown f 19 F s dau yes yes
456   Unknown f 17 F s dau yes yes
457   Unknown m 15 F s son yes yes
458   **Doctor, Unknown** m 14 F s stp-son yes yes
459   **Doctor, Unknown** f 11 F s stp-dau yes yes
460   **Doctor, Unknown** m 6 F s stp-son yes yes
461   **Doctor, Unknown** m 4 F s stp-son yes yes

462   John Frank m 23 F m Head yes yes
463   Lena f 19 F m wife yes yes

464   Jim m 52 F m Head yes yes

Florida Seminoles Indian Census (As of April 1, 1934)

KEY: Census Number Name Sex Age at Last Birthday Tribe (Seminole, unless otherwise stated) Degree of Blood Marital Status Relationship to Head of Family At Jurisdiction where enrolled [Yes or No] (If no, Where) Ward [Yes or No] Allotment, Annuity, and Identification Numbers (if given).

465   Unknown f 62 F m wife yes yes
466   Unknown f 33 F s dau yes yes
467   Little m 31 F s son yes yes
468   Unknown m 29 F s son yes yes
469   Unknown f 26 F s dau yes yes
470   Unknown f 22 F s dau yes yes

471   Mrs. Miami John f 48 F w Head yes yes
472   Willie m 64 F w bro-in-law yes yes
473   Unknown f 14 F s dau yes yes
474   Home Spun m 43 F w nephew yes yes

475   Na-co-tee m 41 F w Head yes yes
476   Unknown m 24 F s son yes yes
477   Unknown f 20 F s dau yes yes
478   Unknown m 18 F s son yes yes
479   Unknown f 16 F s dau yes yes

480   Na-ha m 48 F m Head yes yes
481   Lucy f 56 F m wife yes yes
482   San-tee m 32 F s Head yes yes

483   Tiger m 39 F m Head yes yes
484   Ruby f 36 F m wife yes yes
485   Mar-stook-kee f 17 F s dau yes yes
486   Frank m 15 F s son yes yes
487   Josie m 13 F s son yes yes
488   Cypress m 11 F s son yes yes
489   Harjo m 9 F s son yes yes
490   Unknown f 7 F s dau yes yes
491   Unknown f 3 F s dau yes yes

492   Tiger Boy m 19 F m Head yes yes
493   Martha f 16 F m wife yes yes

TIGERTAIL

494   Ha-ha-wee f 21 F w Head yes yes

Florida Seminoles Indian Census (As of April 1, 1934)

KEY: Census Number Name Sex Age at Last Birthday Tribe (Seminole, unless otherwise stated) Degree of Blood Marital Status Relationship to Head of Family At Jurisdiction where enrolled [Yes or No] (If no, Where) Ward [Yes or No] Allotment, Annuity, and Identification Numbers (if given).

495 Unknown f 3 F s dau yes yes

496 Wilson m 24 F w Head yes yes

497 Unknown f 27 F w Head yes yes
498 Edna f 20 F s sis yes yes
499 Lena f 18 F s sis yes yes
500 Frances f 13 F s sis yes yes

TOMMIE

501 Anna f 78 F w Head yes yes
502 Annie Mae f 40 F s dau yes yes
503 Brownie m 35 F s son yes yes

504 Ben m 51 F m Head yes yes
505 Tudie f 39 F m wife yes yes
506 Mary f 12 F s dau yes yes
507 **Tiger, Missie** f 46 F s sis-in-law yes yes
508 **Parker, Mary** f 12 F s niece yes yes
509 **Parker, Agnes** f 10 F s niece yes yes

510 Frank m 38 F m Head yes yes
511 Sadie f 28 F m wife yes yes
512 Willie Micco m 7 F s son yes yes
513 O-kay m 4 F s son yes yes
514 Joanne f 8/12 F s dau yes yes
515 Jack m 36 F m Head yes yes
516 Charlotte f 29 F m wife yes yes
517 Herbert Hoover m 14 F s son yes yes
518 George m 12 F s son yes yes
519 Fred Smith m 10 F s son yes yes
520 Rosa Lee f 9 F s dau yes yes
521 Odin m 7 F s son yes yes
522 Edward m 5 F s son yes yes
523 Dick m 3 F s son yes yes
524 Unknown f 1 f s dau yes yes

Florida Seminoles Indian Census (As of April 1, 1934)

KEY: Census Number Name Sex Age at Last Birthday Tribe (Seminole, unless otherwise stated) Degree of Blood Marital Status Relationship to Head of Family At Jurisdiction where enrolled [Yes or No] (If no, Where) Ward [Yes or No] Allotment, Annuity, and Identification Numbers (if given).

525	Jim m 38 F m Head yes yes
526	Lo-bee f 30 F m wife yes yes
527	Unknown m 7 F s son yes yes
528	Unknown f 7/12 F s dau yes yes

| 529 | Lady f 30 F w Head yes yes |
| 530 | Baby Morgan f 9 F s dau yes yes |

531	Sam m 29 F m Head yes yes
532	Mary f 20 F m wife yes yes
533	Jimmie m 3 F s son yes yes
534	Sadie f 1 F s dau yes yes

| 535 | Small-pox m 47 F m Head yes yes |
| 536 | Mary f 39 F m wife yes yes |

TONY

537	Capt. Young m 52 F m Head yes yes
538	Unknown f 46 F m wife yes yes
539	Sim-pa-ha-hee f 21 F s dau yes yes
540	**Billie, Unknown** m 32 F s nephew yes yes
541	**Doctor, Jimmie** m 27 F s nephew yes yes
542	**Doctor, Unknown** f 29 F s niece yes yes

TUCKER

543	Chaw-huc-kee f 72 F w Head yes yes
544	Ho-po-thut-kee f 56 F s dau yes yes
545	Mait-kah f 53 F s dau yes yes
546	Sar-thler-na-kee f 30 F s dau yes yes
547	Frank m 28 F s son yes yes
548	**Tiger, Willie** m 28 F s grnd-son yes yes
549	**Tiger, Flora** f 26 F s grnd-dau yes yes

550	Oscar m 38 F m Head yes yes
551	Cot-ner f 35 F m wife yes yes
552	Cos-sum-lak-chee f 19 F s dau yes yes

KEY: Census Number Name Sex Age at Last Birthday Tribe (Seminole, unless otherwise stated)
Degree of Blood Marital Status Relationship to Head of Family At Jurisdiction where enrolled
[Yes or No] (If no, Where) Ward [Yes or No] Allotment, Annuity, and Identification Numbers (if
given).

553   Unknown m 16 F s son yes yes
554   Unknown m 13 F s son yes yes
555   Unknown m 10 F s son yes yes

WALKER

556   Henry m 66 F m Head yes yes
557   Unknown f 54 F m wife yes yes
558   Unknown f 30 F s dau yes yes

559   Wat-cha-kee m 32 F s Head yes yes

WILLIE

560   Frank m 49 F m Head yes yes
561   Ba-shee f 27 F m wife yes yes
562   O-mas-kee m 17 F s son yes yes
563   Yo-pote-ama f 15 F s dau yes yes
564   **Charlie, Pauline** f 8 F s stp-dau yes yes

565   **Jumper, Charlie** m 88 F w Head yes yes

566   Jessie m 34 F m Head yes yes
567   Unknown f 31 F m wife yes yes
568   Unknown f 14 F s dau yes yes
569   Unknown f 13 F s dau yes yes

570   Johnny m 64 F w Head yes yes

571   Sam #1 m 42 F m Head yes yes
572   Unknown f 34 F m wife yes yes
573   Henry m 15 F s son yes yes
574   Walter Roy m 12 F s son yes yes
575   Mary f 9 F s dau yes yes
576   Unknown m 7 F s son yes yes
577   Sam #2 m 18 F m Head yes yes
578   Unknown f 18 F m wife yes yes
579   Unknown m 4 F s son yes yes

KEY: Census Number Name Sex Age at Last Birthday Tribe (Seminole, unless otherwise stated) Degree of Blood Marital Status Relationship to Head of Family At Jurisdiction where enrolled [Yes or No] (If no, Where) Ward [Yes or No] Allotment, Annuity, and Identification Numbers (if given).

580   Unknown f 1 F s dau yes yes

DUPLICATIONS
(Census Number on Last Roll)

BILLIE

36   Grover m 37 - Same as Grover Doctor who died 2 yrs ago and was taken off the roll.

37   Mrs. Grover [Unknown] f 27
38   Unknown m 16
39   Unknown f 14 - Same as Mrs. Grover Doctor and children.

42   Johnson m 19 - Same as Romeo Fewell [Romeo Billie in this census]

BUSTER

87   Addie f 34 - Same as Addie Billie

88   Little f 30 - Same as Frank Charlie's wife

CHARLIE

568   Corinne f 27 - Same as Ba-shee Willie

CYPRESS

110   Henry m 19 - Same as Henry Cypress   [#115 in the old roll]

DOCTOR

153   Hal m 38
154   Annie f 38
155   Lat-i-kee m 15
156   Unknown m 13

KEY: Census Number Name Sex Age at Last Birthday Tribe (Seminole, unless otherwise stated) Degree of Blood Marital Status Relationship to Head of Family At Jurisdiction where enrolled [Yes or No] (If no, Where) Ward [Yes or No] Allotment, Annuity, and Identification Numbers (if given).

157   Unknown f 11
158   Co-sop-cho-tee m 9 - Same as Cologne Doctor and family.

JONES

267   Sam, Sr m 83 - Same as Billie Smith who died this year and was dropped for[sic] the roll.

JUMPER

278   Unknown m 41 - Same as Frank Charlie.

394   Holly m 17 - Same as Harry Jumper.

OSCEOLA

364   Jim Joy m 39
365   Unknown f 36
366   Unknown f 20
367   Unknown f 18
368   Unknown m 15 - Same as Jimmie Druitt and family [Jimmie Druitt Osceola in new roll].

376   Wah-tee f 14 - Same as Little Cypress' wife.

377   Unknown f 9 - Same as Ta-ho-kee Cypress

PLATT

402   Josh m 29 - Same as John Josh.

WILSON

567   Ben m 29 - Same as Ben Wells.

Florida Seminoles Indian Census (As of April 1, 1934)

KEY: Census Number Name Sex Age at Last Birthday Tribe (Seminole, unless otherwise stated) Degree of Blood Marital Status Relationship to Head of Family At Jurisdiction where enrolled [Yes or No] (If no, Where) Ward [Yes or No] Allotment, Annuity, and Identification Numbers (if given).

WRONGFUL ENROLLMENT
(Census Number on Last Roll)

159   Doctor, She-cho-pee m 7

178   Fewell, Unknown m 22

281   Jumper, Unknown f 24

293   Jumper, Unknown f 19
407   Roberts, Lak-kee m 14

DEATHS
(Unreported in Previous Years)

20   Billie, Unknown m 11 Died 2 yrs ago

129   Jumper, Charlie m 68 Died 9 yrs ago

279   Jumper, Miami Charlie m 31 Died 8 yrs ago

325   Morgan, Unknown f 73 Died 3 yrs ago

434   Stewart, Am-a-cjee f 93 Died 6 yrs ago

500   Tommie, Mrs. Charlie f 54 Died 7 yrs ago

Births (As of April 1, 1934)

KEY: 1934 Census Roll Number Parent's Name Child's Given Name Date of Birth Sex Tribe (Seminole, unless otherwise stated) Ward [Yes or No] Degree of Father's Blood Degree of Mother's Blood Degree of Child's Blood At Jurisdiction where enrolled [Yes or No] (If no, Where).

(April 1, 1927 thru March 31, 1928)

460   Doctor, Nae-o-tee Unknown 1928 m yes F F F yes

226   Jim, Willie #3 Unknown 1928 m yes F F F yes

399   Osceola, Wm. McKenley Unknown 1928 m yes F F F yes

(April 1, 1929 thru March 31, 1930)

3   Billie, Albert Unknown 1930 f yes F F F yes

579   Willie, Sam #2 Unknown 1930 m yes F F F yes

(April 1, 1930 thru March 31, 1931)

69   Billie, Yarber Unknown 1931 f yes F F F yes

82   Bowers Lillie Shah-pali-ke-lee 1931 f yes F F F yes

327   Jim, Willie #3 Unknown 1931 m yes F F F yes

(April 1, 1931 thru March 31, 1932)

36   Billie, Kunzie Unknown 1932 m yes F F F yes

42   Billie, Romeo Unknown 1932 m yes F F F yes

46   Billie, Robert Weaver 1932 m yes F F F yes

401   Osceola, Wm McKenley Unknown 1932 f yes F F F yes

(April 1, 1932 thru March 31, 1933)

131   Cypress, Henry Mary 1933 f yes F F F yes

358   Osceola, Cori Unknown 1933 m yes F F F yes

Births (As of April 1, 1934)

KEY: 1934 Census Roll Number Parent's Name Child's Given Name Date of Birth Sex Tribe (Seminole, unless otherwise stated) Ward [Yes or No] Degree of Father's Blood Degree of Mother's Blood Degree of Child's Blood At Jurisdiction where enrolled [Yes or No] (If no, Where).

524   Tommie, Jack Unknown 1933 f yes F F F yes

580   Willie, Sam #2 Unknown 1933 f yes F F F yes

(April 1, 1933 thru March 31, 1934)

Billie, Mrs. John Unknown 5-10-1933 m yes F F F yes

4   Billie, Albert Unknown 6-3-1933 f yes F F F yes

19   Billie, Jimmie #1 Unknown 10-1-1933 m yes F F F yes

119   Cypress, Frank Unknown 9-30-1933 m yes F F F yes

128   Cypress, Johnny Unknown 6-30-1933 f yes F F F yes

154   Dixie, Susie Unknown 7-15-1933 m F ¾ 7/8 yes

171   Doctor, Wilson Unknown 6-6-1933 m yes F F F yes

Doctor, Little Unknown 12 25-1933 f yes F F F yes

219   Jim, Willie #2 Unknown 10-1-1933 m yes F F F yes

Johns, Lillie Unknown 7-6-1933 m White F ½ yes

Jumper, Lobi Unknown 5-2-1933 f yes F F F yes

278   Jumper, John Mary 9-26-1933 f yes F F F yes

310   Micco, Charlie Unknown 7-23-1933 m yes F F F yes

376   Osceola, Jimmie D Unknown 10-1-1933 m yes F F F yes

514   Tommie, Frank Joanna 9-17-1933 f yes F F F yes

528   Tommie, Jim Unknown 10-19-1933 f yes F F F yes

Births (As of April 1, 1934)

Tucker, Oscar Unknown 11-1-1933 m yes F F F yes

Deaths (Between April 1, 1924, and March 31, 1934)

KEY: Census Number and Year Name Death Date Age at Death Sex Tribe (Seminole, unless otherwise stated) Ward [Yes or No] Degree of Blood Cause of Death At Jurisdiction where enrolled [Yes or No] (If no, Where).

1   1933 Billie, Mrs. Corn 4-9-1934 33 f yes F Cancer ?

8   1933 Billie, Unknown 1-13-1934 ¼ f yes F Bronchitis ?

16   1933 Billie, Girtman 12-28-1933 37 m yes F Auto wreck ?

------ Billie, Unknown [Baby of Mrs. John] 1-5-1934 8/12 m yes F Pneumonia ?

------ Doctor, Unknown [Baby of Little] 1-15-1934 4 wks f yes F Unknown ?

201 1933 Gopher, Unknown 1-4-1934 3 f yes F Flu ?

------ Johns, Unknown [Baby of Lillie] 8-28-1933 6 wks m yes ½ Whooping cough ?

------ Jumper, Unknown [Baby of Lobi] 9-27-1933 4/12 f yes F Bronchitis ?

386 1933 Osceola, Lena 10-28-1933 18 f yes F Child birth ?

383 1933 Osceola, Pal-i-kee 12-28-1933 16 m yes F Auto wreck ?

408 1933 Smith, Billie 7-26-1933 83 m yes F Old age ?

481 1933 Tigertail, Charlie 12-19-1933 63 m yes F Drowned - auto wreck ?

------ Tucker, Unknown [Baby of Oscar] 12-26-1933 2/12 m yes F Pneumonia ?

Never listed Doctor, Mrs. John 6-15-1933 35 f yes F TB

(April 1, 1924 thru March 31, 1933)

129 1933 Jumper, Charlie 1925 59 m yes F Unknown ?

Deaths (Between April 1, 1924, and March 31, 1934)

279   1933 Jumper, Miami Charlie 1926 23 m yes F Unknown ?

500   1933 Tommie, Mrs. Charlie 1927 47 f yes F Unknown ?

434   1933 Stewart, Am-a-chee 1928 87 f yes F Unknown ?

325   1933 Morgan, Unknown 1931 70 f yes F Unknown ?

 20   1933 Billie, Unknown 1932 9 m yes F Unknown ?

BIRTHS (Between January 1 and December 31, 1936)

9 Billie, Frances 1-4-36 f yes F F F yes

DBE Billie, Unknown 9-26-36 f yes F F F yes

DBE Billie, Unknown 9-27-36 m yes F F F yes

DBE Billie, Unknown 9-27-36 f yes F F F yes

189 Fewell, Martha 3-26-36 f yes F F F yes

240 Jim Unknown 12-1-36 f yes F F F yes

264 Johns, Archie 7-24-36 m yes F F F yes

298 Jumper, Allison 4-19-36 m yes F F F yes

331 Motloe, Ya-co-see 1-4-36 f yes F F F yes

391 Osceola, Capt. Joe Don 12-20-36 m yes F F F yes

433 Smith, Unknown 3-25-36 f yes F ¾ 7/8 yes

434 Smith, Unknown 3-25-36 f yes F ¾ 7/8 yes

535 Tommie, Oct-sa-ta-kee 5-24-36 f yes F F F yes

523 Tommie, Unknown 11-1-36 f yes F F F yes

553 Tucker, Unknown 5-7-36 f yes F F F yes

582 Willie, Calvin 8-25-36 m yes F F F yes

586 Willie, Unknown 2-13-26 f yes F F F yes

BIRTHS (Between January 1 and December 31, 1936)

KEY: Census Number (If Died Before Enrollment, DBE will be inserted instead of number) Name Date of Birth Sex Tribe (Seminole, unless otherwise stated) Ward [Yes or No] Degree of Father's Blood Degree of Mother's Blood Degree of Child's Blood At Jurisdiction where enrolled [Yes or No] (If no, Where).

UNREPORTED BIRTHS
(January 1 thru December 31, 1933)

31   Billie, Mary 1933 f yes F F F yes

DBE   Johns, Rosa 1933 f yes White F ½ yes

(January 1 thru December 31, 1935)

490   Tiger, Lum-kee 9-20-1935 m yes F F F yes

552   Tucker, Billie 1935 m yes F F F yes

OMITTED FROM PREVIOUS ROLLS
(Number Name Sex Age at Last Birthday
Seminole Tribe - only information given)

36   Billie, John m 33

39   Billie, Johnnie m 28

26   Billie, Thee-lo-kee m 6

422   Smith, George m 9

DBE   Smith, Sampson m 15

471   Tiger, Shee-ma-hat-thee f 27

492   Tigertail, John White m 22

527   Tommie, Jimmie m 7

Florida Seminoles Indian Census (As of January 1, 1937)

KEY: Census Number Name Sex Age at Last Birthday Tribe (Seminole, unless otherwise stated) Degree of Blood Marital Status Relationship to Head of Family At Jurisdiction where enrolled [Yes or No] (If no, Where) Ward [Yes or No] Allotment, Annuity, and Identification Numbers (if given).

BILLIE

1	Albert	m	37	F	m	Head	yes	yes
2	Willie	f	33	F	m	wife	yes	yes
3	Marion	f	7	F	s	dau	yes	yes

1 Albert m 37 F m Head yes yes
2 Willie f 33 F m wife yes yes
3 Marion f 7 F s dau yes yes

4 Charlie m 56 F m Head yes yes
5 Mona f 53 F m wife yes yes
6 Maggie f 25 F s dau yes yes

7 Charlie m 21 F m Head yes yes
8 So-ho-wa-kee f 38 F m wife yes yes
9 Frances f 11/12 (1-5-36) F s dau yes yes
10 **Doctor, Josie** f 14 F s stp-dau yes yes
11 **Doctor, Boy** m 9 F s stp-son yes yes
12 **Doctor, Billie** m 7 F s stp-son yes yes

13 Chestnut m 31 F m Head yes yes
14 To-li-kee f 31 F m wife yes yes

15 Cowboy m 27 F w Head yes yes

16 Frank m 21 F m Head yes yes
17 Peggy f 19 F m wife yes yes
18 Unknown f 2 (8-2-34) F s dau yes yes

19 George m 19 F m Head yes yes [Died 11-20-37]
20 Mable f 20 F m wife yes yes

21 Goodman m 19 F s Head yes yes

22 Homespun m 46 F w Head yes yes

23 Ingram m 42 F m Head yes yes
24 Stim-a-thee f 41 F m wife yes yes
25 Unknown f 10 F s dau yes yes
26 Thee-lo-kee m 6 F s son yes yes

Florida Seminoles Indian Census (As of January 1, 1937)

KEY: Census Number Name Sex Age at Last Birthday Tribe (Seminole, unless otherwise stated) Degree of Blood Marital Status Relationship to Head of Family At Jurisdiction where enrolled [Yes or No] (If no, Where) Ward [Yes or No] Allotment, Annuity, and Identification Numbers (if given).

27   Jimmie m 37 F m Head yes yes
28   Unknown f 31 F m wife yes yes

29   Jimmie m 23 F m Head yes yes
30   Cla-sa-he-yee f 18 F m wife yes yes
31   Mary f 3 F s dau yes yes

32   John m 31 F m Head yes yes
33   Ma-wee-he-lee f 43 F m wife yes yes
34   Homer m 8 F s son yes yes
35   Maxie m 4 (12-24-32) F s son yes yes

36   John m 33 F m Head yes yes
37   Lena f 29 F m wife yes yes

38   John Phillip m 31 F s Head yes yes

39   Johnnie m 28 F m Head yes yes
40   Tommie f 24 F m wife yes yes
41   Effie f 12 F s stp-dau yes yes
42   Agnes f 10 F s stp-dau yes yes

43   Josie m 51 F m Head yes yes
44   Unknown f 51 F m wife yes yes

45   Julia f 32 F w Head yes yes
46   **Smith, Louise** f 7 F s dau yes yes
47   **Smith, Jim Stewart** m 4 F s son yes yes

48   Kunzie m 41 F m Head yes yes
49   Addie f 38 F m wife yes yes
50   Unknown f 15 F s dau yes yes
51   Unknown m 5 F s son yes yes

52   Little Charlie m 40 F m Head yes yes
53   Chi-ki-kee f 55 F m wife yes yes

54   Mary f 40 F w Head yes yes

Florida Seminoles Indian Census (As of January 1, 1937)

KEY: Census Number Name Sex Age at Last Birthday Tribe (Seminole, unless otherwise stated) Degree of Blood Marital Status Relationship to Head of Family At Jurisdiction where enrolled [Yes or No] (If no, Where) Ward [Yes or No] Allotment, Annuity, and Identification Numbers (if given).

55	Robert m 36 F m Head yes yes	
56	Josie f 37 F m wife yes yes	
57	Milton m 7 F s son yes yes	
58	Weaver m 5 F s son yes yes	
59	Alfred m 1 (7-30-35) F s son yes yes	
60	Romeo m 29 F m Head yes yes	
61	Little f 24 F m wife yes yes	
62	Unknown m 5 F s son yes yes	
63	Rosalie f 23 F w Head yes yes	
64	Edna f 19 F s niece yes yes	
65	Johnson m 17 F s nephew yes yes	
66	Johnny m 15 F s nephew yes yes	
67	Larry m 12 F s nephew yes yes	
68	Unknown f 10 F s niece yes yes	
69	Peggy f 6 F s niece yes yes	
70	Wat-see f 47 F w Head yes yes	
71	Effie f 14 F s dau yes yes	
72	Frances f 11 F s dau yes yes	
73	Paul m 10 F s son yes yes	
74	Willie m 48 F w Head yes yes	
75	Wilson m 35 F w Head yes yes	

BOWERS

76	Lillie f 41 F w Head yes yes
77	**Buster, Bessie** f 12 ½ s dau yes yes
78	Elizabeth f 6 F s dau yes yes
79	**Willie, Ruby** f 46 F w sister yes yes
80	**Willie, Little** f 7 (1-15-29) F s niece yes yes

BOWLEGS

81	Billie m 70 ½ w Head yes yes
82	**Tucker, Lewis** m 52 ½ s bro yes yes

133

Florida Seminoles Indian Census (As of January 1, 1937)

KEY: Census Number Name Sex Age at Last Birthday Tribe (Seminole, unless otherwise stated) Degree of Blood Marital Status Relationship to Head of Family At Jurisdiction where enrolled [Yes or No] (If no, Where) Ward [Yes or No] Allotment, Annuity, and Identification Numbers (if given).

83   **Pearce, Lucy** f 55 ½ w sis yes yes
84   **Pearce, Ada** f 26 ¾ s niece yes yes
85   **Pearce, Anna** f 24 ¾ s niece yes yes

86   Eli Morgan m 43 ¾ m Head yes yes
87   Lena f 37 F m wife yes yes
88   **Bowers, Andrew Jackson** m 28 F w stp-son yes yes
89   **Bowers, Lydee** f 25 F s stp-dau yes yes
90   **Bowers, Dick** m 21 F s stp-son yes yes
91   **Bowers, Ka-pik-cha-ha-che** m 19 F s stp-son yes yes
92   **Bowers, Unknown** m 17 F s stp-son yes yes
93   **Bowers, Unknown** m 15 F s stp-son yes yes
94   **Bowers, Unknown** m 13 F s stp-son yes yes

BUCK

95   John m 39 F w Head yes yes

BUSTER

96   Billie m 70 F w Head yes yes

97   Billie m 30 F s Head yes yes

98   Charlie m 65 F w Head yes yes

99   Johnny m 40 F w Head yes yes

100   Johnny m 47 F m Head yes yes
101   In-git-tah-yee f 49 F m wife yes yes
102   So-wah-ho-yee f 19 F s stp-dau yes yes
103   Unknown m 10 F s son yes yes
104   Unknown f 8 F s dau yes yes
105   Lois f 30 F s Head yes yes

106   Nellie f 86 F w Head yes yes   [Died 6-5-37]
107   Annie f 68 F s dau yes yes
108   Yek-am-kah f 38 F s dau yes yes

Florida Seminoles Indian Census (As of January 1, 1937)

KEY: Census Number Name Sex Age at Last Birthday Tribe (Seminole, unless otherwise stated) Degree of Blood Marital Status Relationship to Head of Family At Jurisdiction where enrolled [Yes or No] (If no, Where) Ward [Yes or No] Allotment, Annuity, and Identification Numbers (if given).

109   Tom m 18 F m Head yes yes
110   Ruby f 19 F m wife yes yes

CHARLIE

111   Frank m 26 F m Head yes yes
112   Carrie f 25 F m wife yes yes

CLAY

113   Mrs. Henry f 47 F w Head yes yes
114   Abraham Lincoln m 39 F s stp-son yes yes
115   Ta-la-kee f 25 F s dau yes yes
116   Nac-ho-mee f 17 F s dau yes yes
117   Jack Johnson m 33 F m Head yes yes
118   Ruby f 29 F m wife yes yes
119   Bob m 1 (3-28-35) F s son yes yes

CYPRESS

120   Charlie m 66 F m Head yes yes
121   Lee f 53 F m wife yes yes
122   Ada f 11 F s dau yes yes
123   Stanley Hanson m 9 F s son yes yes

124   Mrs. Frank f 21 F w Head yes yes
125   Kenley Carson m 3 (9-30-33) F s son yes yes

126   Futch m 61 F m Head yes yes
127   Unknown f 50 F m wife yes yes
128   Cin-ta-chee-no-chee m 13 F s son yes yes
129   Unknown m 11 F s son yes yes

130   Johnnie m 35 F m Head yes yes
131   Mary f 33 F m wife yes yes
132   Stanley Hansee m 10 F s son yes yes
133   Buck m 9 (1-1-28) F s son yes yes
134   Julia f 3 (6-30-33) F s dau yes yes

135

KEY: Census Number Name Sex Age at Last Birthday Tribe (Seminole, unless otherwise stated) Degree of Blood Marital Status Relationship to Head of Family At Jurisdiction where enrolled [Yes or No] (If no, Where) Ward [Yes or No] Allotment, Annuity, and Identification Numbers (if given).

135   Gene Sterling m 1 (10-30-35) F s son yes yes   [Died 2-28-37]

136   Henry m 32 F m Head yes yes
137   Annie f 21 F m wife yes yes
138   Mary f 4 F s dau yes yes

139   Little m 31 F m Head yes yes
140   Mary f 25 F m wife yes yes
141   Unknown m 3 (5-6-33) F s son yes yes
142   Unknown f 2 (10-20-34) F s dau yes yes

143   Whitney m 57 F m Head yes yes
144   Sally f 45 F m wife yes yes
145   Anna f 23 F s dau yes yes
146   Betty Mae f 21 F s dau yes yes
147   Junior m 18 F s son yes yes
148   Mary f 15 F s dau yes yes
149   Jimmie m 14 F s son yes yes
150   Wilson m 49 F m Head yes yes
151   Ruby f 39 F m wife yes yes
152   Lena f 21 F s dau yes yes
153   Marion f 20 F s dau yes yes
154   Belle f 19 F s dau yes yes
155   Frank m 14 F s son yes yes

DIXIE

156   Charlie m 65 ½ m Head yes yes
157   Jim-Sling f 60 F m wife yes yes
158   Walter Huff m 32 ¾ s son yes yes
159   Susie f 27 ¾ w dau yes yes
160   Samson m 15 ¾ s son yes yes
161   Unknown m 3 (7-15-33) 7/8 s grnd-son yes yes

DOCTOR

162   Cologne m 41 F m Head yes yes
163   Unknown f 36 F m wife yes yes

Florida Seminoles Indian Census (As of January 1, 1937)

KEY: Census Number Name Sex Age at Last Birthday Tribe (Seminole, unless otherwise stated) Degree of Blood Marital Status Relationship to Head of Family At Jurisdiction where enrolled [Yes or No] (If no, Where) Ward [Yes or No] Allotment, Annuity, and Identification Numbers (if given).

164	Unknown m 21 F s son yes yes
165	Unknown m 17 F s son yes yes
166	Unknown m 14 F s son yes yes
167	Unknown f 7 F s dau yes yes

| 168 | Jim Henry m 17 F m Head yes yes |
| 169 | Mattie f 17 F m wife yes yes |

170	Little m 69 F m Head yes yes
171	Mamie f 41 F m wife yes yes
172	Tommie m 17 F s son yes yes

173	Unknown f 56 F w Head yes yes
174	Unknown m 18 F s son yes yes
175	Unknown m 16 F s son yes yes
176	Unknown f 13 F s dau yes yes

177	Wilson m 37 F m Head yes yes
178	O-sha-fish-shee f 38 F m wife yes yes
179	Unknown m 8 F s son yes yes
180	Unknown m 3 (6-6-33) F s son yes yes

FEWELL

181	Charlie m 61 F m Head yes yes
182	Li-chee f 48 f m wife yes yes
183	Lidly m 24 F s son yes yes
184	Mary f 22 F s dau yes yes
185	Maggie f 13 F s dau yes yes

186	Johnny m 37 F m Head yes yes
187	Eula f 33 F m wife yes yes
188	Juanita f 12 F s dau yes yes
189	Martha f 9/12 (3-26-36) F s dau yes yes

Florida Seminoles Indian Census (As of January 1, 1937)

KEY: Census Number Name Sex Age at Last Birthday Tribe (Seminole, unless otherwise stated)
Degree of Blood Marital Status Relationship to Head of Family At Jurisdiction where enrolled
[Yes or No] (If no, Where) Ward [Yes or No] Allotment, Annuity, and Identification Numbers (if
given).

FRANK

190   Miami m 57 F s Head yes yes   [Died prior to 1937 - Date
       unknown]

FRAZIER

191   Bird m 32 F w Head yes yes

GOPHER

192   Jim m 67 F w Head yes yes
193   Ada f 38 F s dau yes yes

194   Lucy Tiger f 54 F w Head yes yes
195   Willie m 24 F s son yes yes
196   John Henry m 21 F s son yes yes
197   Annie f 20 F s dau yes yes
198   Lena f 19 F s dau yes yes

HENRY

199   Jim m 47 F w Head yes yes

200   Tim-a-kee [Mrs. Jim] f 37 F w Head yes yes
201   Unknown f 16 F s dau yes yes
202   Unknown m 14 F s son yes yes

HUFF

203   Alice f 21 F w Head yes yes
204   So-fa-lay-hee f 4 (9-3-32) F s dau yes yes
205   Frances f 1 (7-16-35) F s dau yes yes

206   Frank m 24 F m Head yes yes
207   Mary f 23 F m wife yes yes

Florida Seminoles Indian Census (As of January 1, 1937)

KEY: Census Number Name Sex Age at Last Birthday Tribe (Seminole, unless otherwise stated) Degree of Blood Marital Status Relationship to Head of Family At Jurisdiction where enrolled [Yes or No] (If no, Where) Ward [Yes or No] Allotment, Annuity, and Identification Numbers (if given).

208   Sam m 54 F w Head yes yes

JIM

209   Frank m 37 F m Head yes yes
210   Annie f 24 F m wife yes yes
211   Unknown f 1 (3-16-35) F s dau yes yes

212   Johnnie m 40 F m Head yes yes
213   Mon-ta-kee f 35 F m wife yes yes
214   Unknown f 15 F s dau yes yes
215   Unknown m 13 F s son yes yes
216   Ah-po-kee f 23 F s niece yes yes
217   Unknown m 19 F s nephew yes yes

218   Unknown f 43 F s Head yes yes

219   Wa-ti-kee f 65 F w Head yes yes   [Died 6-22-37]
220   Boy m 35 F s son yes yes
221   Buffalo Bill m 32 F s son yes yes
222   Unknown f 18 F s dau yes yes

223   Willie m 47 F m Head yes yes
224   Unknown f 44 F m wife yes yes
225   Unknown f 17 F s dau yes yes
226   Unknown f 14 F s dau yes yes

227   Willie m 39 F m Head yes yes
228   Hick-chi-he-chlee f 26 F m wife yes yes
229   Unknown f 16 F s dau yes yes
230   Unknown f 13 F s dau yes yes
231   Unknown f 11 F s dau yes yes

232   Willie m 40 F m Head yes yes
233   Unknown f 35 F m wife yes yes
234   Unknown m 18 F s son yes yes
235   Unknown m 16 F s son yes yes
236   Unknown f 14 F s dau yes yes

KEY: Census Number Name Sex Age at Last Birthday Tribe (Seminole, unless otherwise stated) Degree of Blood Marital Status Relationship to Head of Family At Jurisdiction where enrolled [Yes or No] (If no, Where) Ward [Yes or No] Allotment, Annuity, and Identification Numbers (if given).

237   Unknown f 11 F s dau yes yes
238   Unknown m 9 F s son yes yes
239   Unknown m 6 F s son yes yes
240   Unknown f 1/12 (12-1-36) F s dau yes   yes

JIMMIE

241   Little m 37 F m Head yes yes
242   Unknown f 35 F m wife yes yes
243   Unknown f 19 F s dau yes yes
244   Unknown m 17 F s son yes yes

JOHNNY

245   Kir-kee m 42 F s Head yes yes
246   Sar-pi-kul-ker f 45 F s sister yes yes
247   Ma-har f 44 F s sister yes yes

JOHNS

248   Annie f 71 F w Head yes yes
249   Dolly f 39 F s dau yes yes
250   Oscar m 35 F s son yes yes
251   Arnie f 31 F s dau yes yes
252   Lizzie f 29 F s dau yes yes
253   Tobie m 27 F s son yes yes
254   Ka-see-ha-chee f 25 F s dau yes yes
255   Lillie f 21 F s dau yes yes
256   Mamie f 18 F s dau yes yes
257   Lena f 15 F s dau yes yes
258   Lottie f 7 ½ s grnd-dau yes yes
259   Lucy f 4 (11-30-32) ½ s grnd-dau yes yes

260   Unknown m 2 (5-28-34) ½ s grnd-son yes yes
                              [Died prior to 1937-Date unknown]
261   Frank m 1 (7-7-35) F s grnd-son yes yes

262   Barfield m 23 F m Head yes yes

Florida Seminoles Indian Census (As of January 1, 1937)

KEY: Census Number Name Sex Age at Last Birthday Tribe (Seminole, unless otherwise stated) Degree of Blood Marital Status Relationship to Head of Family At Jurisdiction where enrolled [Yes or No] (If no, Where) Ward [Yes or No] Allotment, Annuity, and Identification Numbers (if given).

263   Susie f 16 F m wife yes yes
264   Archie m 5/12 (7-24-36) F s son yes yes
265   Ernic f 49 F s Head yes yes

266   Sheela Hillard f 39 F w Head yes yes
267   Maud f 19 F s dau yes yes
268   Joe m 16 F s son yes yes

JONES

269   Sam m 43 F m Head yes yes
270   Missie Stick f 41 F m wife yes yes
271   Free f 23 F s dau yes yes
272   Henry m 20 F s son yes yes
273   Willie m 17 F s son yes yes
274   Unknown f 15 F s dau yes yes
275   Unknown f 13 F s dau yes yes
276   Unknown f 11 F s dau yes yes
277   Unknown f 9 F s dau yes yes
278   Unknown m 8 F s son yes yes
279   Unknown m 4 (5-1-32) F s son yes yes

JOSH

280   John m 27 ¾ m Head yes yes
281   Henley Dennie f 30 F m wife yes yes
282   Fi-kee f 75 ½ w mother yes yes

JUMPER

283   Chief Charlie m 30 F m Head yes yes
284   Rosalie f 40 F m wife yes yes

285   Harry m 26 F m Head yes yes
286   Tommie f 28 F m wife yes yes
287   Scott Wee-wee m 4 (6-2-32) F s son yes yes
288   Mary f 1 (6-20-35) F s dau yes yes
289   John m 27 F m Head yes yes

KEY: Census Number Name Sex Age at Last Birthday Tribe (Seminole, unless otherwise stated) Degree of Blood Marital Status Relationship to Head of Family At Jurisdiction where enrolled [Yes or No] (If no, Where) Ward [Yes or No] Allotment, Annuity, and Identification Numbers (if given).

290	Lena	f	25	F	m	wife	yes	yes	
291	Mary	f	3 (9-26-33)	F	s	dau	yes	yes	
292	Billie	m	1 (6-28-35)	F	s	son	yes	yes	
293	Johnny	m	50	F	m	Head	yes	yes	
294	Unknown	f	57	F	m	wife	yes	yes	
295	Rosy	f	30	F	s	dau	yes	yes	

296	Josie	m	32	F	m	Head	yes	yes	
297	Pocahontas	f	28	F	m	wife	yes	yes	
298	Allison	m	8/12 (4-19-36)	F	s	son	yes	yes	
299	**Huff, George**	m	8 (11-8-28)	F	s	stp-son	yes	yes	

300	Katy	f	31	F	w	Head	yes	yes	
301	Moses	m	10	F	s	son	yes	yes	
302	Lura	f	5 (11-13-31)	F	s	dau	yes	yes	

303	Little Charlie	m	55	F	m	Head	yes	yes	
304	Sally	f	46	F	m	wife	yes	yes	
305	Henry	m	15	F	s	son	yes	yes	

306	Mrs. Squirrel	f	57	F	w	Head	yes	yes	
307	Stem-i-he-ooh	f	37	F	s	dau	yes	yes	
308	Unknown	m	33	F	s	son	yes	yes	

309	Willie	m	67	F	s	Head	yes	yes	

MARCEY

310	Tulu	102	F	w	Head	yes	yes	[Died prior to 1937 - Date unknown]

MICCO

311	Charlie	m	45	F	m	Head	yes	yes	
312	Was-wah-kee	f	37	F	m	wife	yes	yes	
313	Little Charlie	m	21	F	s	son	yes	yes	
314	Unknown	f	16	F	s	dau	yes	yes	
315	Alice	f	13	F	s	dau	yes	yes	
316	Little Jack	m	7 (9-1-29)	F	s	son	yes	yes	

KEY: Census Number Name Sex Age at Last Birthday Tribe (Seminole, unless otherwise stated) Degree of Blood Marital Status Relationship to Head of Family At Jurisdiction where enrolled [Yes or No] (If no, Where) Ward [Yes or No] Allotment, Annuity, and Identification Numbers (if given).

317   Unknown m 3 (7-23-33) F s son yes yes

318   Oscar m 40 F m Head yes yes
319   To-chee f 37 F m wife yes yes
320   Unknown f 19 F s dau yes yes
321   Unknown f 17 F s dau yes yes
322   Unknown f 15 F s dau yes yes
323   Unknown f 13 F s dau yes yes
324   Unknown m 11 F s son yes yes

MORGAN

325   Jake m 41 F w Head yes yes
326   **Biglow, Mamie** f 32 F w sister yes yes
327   **Biglow, Lauderdale** f 4 (12-1-32) F s niece yes yes

MOTLOE

328   Jack m 43 F m Head yes yes
329   Belle f 41 F m wife yes yes
330   Louise f 4 (12-2-32) F s dau yes yes
331   Ya-co-see f 11/12 (1-4-36) F s dau yes yes
332   Ollie f 10 F s stp-dau yes yes

333   John m 37 F m Head yes yes
334   Les-hee f 24 F m wife yes yes
335   Jennie f 52 F w cousin yes yes
336   Billie m 81 F w father yes yes   [Died 6-15-37]

OSCEOLA

337   Billie m 45 F m Head yes yes
338   Ruby f 41 F m wife yes yes
339   Tak-hat-a-see f 26 F s dau yes yes
340   Unknown f 23 F s dau yes yes
341   Che-ho-kee m 21 F s son yes yes
342   Unknown f 19 F s dau yes yes
343   Unknown m 17 F s son yes yes

KEY: Census Number Name Sex Age at Last Birthday Tribe (Seminole, unless otherwise stated) Degree of Blood Marital Status Relationship to Head of Family At Jurisdiction where enrolled [Yes or No] (If no, Where) Ward [Yes or No] Allotment, Annuity, and Identification Numbers (if given).

344 Unknown m 15 F s son yes yes
345 Jimmie m 13 F s son yes yes

346 Billie m 46 F w Head yes yes
347 Lena f 19 F s dau yes yes
348 Mattie f 17 F s dau yes yes
349 Jimmie m 15 F s son yes yes
350 **Johns, Doctor** m 39 F w bro-in-law yes yes
351 **Johns, Bartman** m 16 F s nephew yes yes
352 Unknown f 12 F s niece yes yes

353 Charlie m 30 F w Head yes yes
354 Unknown m 10 F s son yes yes
355 Unknown f 9 F s dau yes yes

356 Cori m 32 F m Head yes yes
357 Juanita f 28 F m wife yes yes
358 Unknown f 9 (8-29-27) F s dau yes yes
359 Unknown m 7 F s son yes yes
360 Pattis m 4 F s son yes yes
361 Unknown m 1 (4-25-35) F s son yes yes

362 Frank m 20 F m Head yes yes
363 Ruby f 22 F m wife yes yes
364 Ot-to-lee m 1 (7-21-35) F s son yes yes

365 George m 57 F m Head yes yes
366 Non-for-mee f 46 F m wife yes yes
367 Henry m 23 F s son yes yes
368 William Buck m 18 F s son yes yes
369 Unknown f 17 F s dau yes yes

370 Jimmie m 89 F w Head yes yes
371 Harjo m 21 F s son yes yes
372 Robert m 19 F s son yes yes
373 Stuman m 13 F s son yes yes
374 Billie m 11 F s son yes yes

144

Florida Seminoles Indian Census (As of January 1, 1937)

KEY: Census Number Name Sex Age at Last Birthday Tribe (Seminole, unless otherwise stated) Degree of Blood Marital Status Relationship to Head of Family At Jurisdiction where enrolled [Yes or No] (If no, Where) Ward [Yes or No] Allotment, Annuity, and Identification Numbers (if given).

375	Jimmie Druitt m 37 F m Head yes yes
376	Unknown f 37 F m wife yes yes
377	Billie m 18 F s son yes yes
378	Mary f 17 F s dau yes yes
379	Unknown m 13 F s son yes yes
380	Max Bill m 7 F s son yes yes
381	Unknown f 3 (10-3-33) F s dau yes yes

382	John m 66 F m Head yes yes
383	Ida f 57 F m wife yes yes
384	Jack m 20 F s son yes yes
385	**Frazier, John Bird** m 10 F s grnd-son yes yes
386	**Frazier, Henry Bird** m 7 F s grnd-son yes yes

387	John m 55 F m Head yes yes
388	Unknown f 55 F m wife yes yes

389	Richard m 31 F m Head yes yes
390	Anna f 24 F m wife yes yes
391	Capt. Joe Don m ? (12-20-36) F s son yes yes
392	Francis m 3 (10-25-33) F s son yes yes

393	Mrs. Robert f 25 F w Head yes yes
394	Roy Nash m 6 F s son yes yes

395	William McKinley m 42 F m Head yes yes
396	To-wee f 35 F m wife yes yes
397	Homer m 20 F s son yes yes
398	Mittie f 18 F s dau yes yes
399	Mike m 16 F s son yes yes
400	Douglas m 13 F s son yes yes
401	Howard m 10 F s son yes yes
402	John A m 0 F s son yes yes
403	William McKinley, Jr m 6 F s son yes yes
404	Agnes f 5 F s dau yes yes

405	Wit-kee f 45 F w Head yes yes
406	Unknown f 28 F s dau yes yes

KEY: Census Number Name Sex Age at Last Birthday Tribe (Seminole, unless otherwise stated) Degree of Blood Marital Status Relationship to Head of Family At Jurisdiction where enrolled [Yes or No] (If no, Where) Ward [Yes or No] Allotment, Annuity, and Identification Numbers (if given).

407   Unknown m 22 F s son yes yes

PARKER

408   Argyle m 38 F s Head yes yes
409   Millie f 41 F s sister yes yes

410   Courtney f 43 F w Head yes yes
411   Parker, Maud f 4 (12-11-32) F s dau yes yes

412   Dan m 43 F m Head yes yes
413   Tommie f 38 F m wife yes yes
414   **Jim, John** m 15 F s stp-son yes yes

PEACOCK

415   Charlie m 42 F s Head yes yes

PRETTY

416   Old m 69 F w Head yes yes

ROBERTS

417   Elsie f 20 F s Head yes yes
418   Billie m 18 F s brother yes yes

SMITH

419   Dick m 56 F w Head yes yes
420   Judge Fee m 21 F s son yes yes
421   Ruby f 20 F s dau yes yes
422   George m 9 F s son yes yes

423   Jack m 15 F m Head yes yes
424   Leona f 18 F m wife yes yes

425   Morgan m 37 F w Head yes yes

KEY: Census Number Name Sex Age at Last Birthday Tribe (Seminole, unless otherwise stated) Degree of Blood Marital Status Relationship to Head of Family At Jurisdiction where enrolled [Yes or No] (If no, Where) Ward [Yes or No] Allotment, Annuity, and Identification Numbers (if given).

426	Mrs. Billie f 82 F w mother yes yes
427	Dollie f 54 F s sister yes yes
428	Gullie f 39 F s sister yes yes
429	Tom m 48 F m Head yes yes
430	Stella f 37 ¾ m wife yes yes
431	Unknown f 10 7/8 s dau yes yes
432	Unknown m 8 7/8 s son yes yes
433	Unknown f 9/12 (3-27-36) 7/8 s dau yes yes
434	Unknown f 9/12 (3-27-36) 7/8 s dau yes yes

SNOW

435	Sampson m 41 F m Head yes yes
436	Mak-ka-na-kee f 36 F m wife yes yes
437	Bob m 13 F s son yes yes
438	Fes-a-ha-liza f 7 (8-1-29) F s dau yes yes
439	He-sha-ez-a f 4 (4-1-32) F s dau yes yes

STEWART

440	Billie m 62 F m Head yes yes
441	Susie f 58 F m wife yes yes
442	Fannie f 35 F s dau yes yes
443	**Charlie, Big** m 54 F s bro-in-law yes yes

TIGER

444	Ada f 38 F w Head yes yes
445	Betty Mae f 15 (4-7-21) ½ s dau yes yes
446	Howard m 13 ½ s son yes yes
447	Mary f 77 F w mother yes yes
448	Brown m 47 F w Head yes yes
449	Charlie m 55 F w Head yes yes
450	Cuffney m 59 F m Head yes yes

Florida Seminoles Indian Census (As of January 1, 1937)

KEY: Census Number Name Sex Age at Last Birthday Tribe (Seminole, unless otherwise stated) Degree of Blood Marital Status Relationship to Head of Family At Jurisdiction where enrolled [Yes or No] (If no, Where) Ward [Yes or No] Allotment, Annuity, and Identification Numbers (if given).

451   Unknown f 55 F m wife yes yes
452   Unknown f 13 F s stp-dau yes yes

453   Doctor m 58 F w Head yes yes

454   Emma f 46 F w Head yes yes
455   Poland Poole f 27 F s dau yes yes

456   Frank m 46 F w Head yes yes
457   Mary f 20 F s dau yes yes
458   Henry m 18 F s son yes yes
459   Ales-ah-po-hee f 4/12 (8-12-35) F s grnd-dau yes yes

460   John Frank m 26 F m Head yes yes
461   Lena f 22 F m wife yes yes

462   John Poole m 25 F m Head yes yes
463   Camilla f 19 F m wife yes yes

464   Jim m 55 F m Head yes yes   [Died 6-8-37]
465   Unknown f 65 F m wife yes yes   [Died 9-17-37]
466   Unknown f 36 F s dau yes yes
467   Unknown m 32 F s son yes yes
468   Unknown f 29 F s dau yes yes
469   Unknown f 25 F s dau yes yes   [Died 9-17-37]

470   Little m 34 F m Head yes yes
471   Shee-ma-hat-thee f 27 F m wife yes yes
472   Unknown f 1 (8-14-35) F s dau yes yes

473   Na-co-tee m 44 F w Head yes yes
474   Unknown m 27 F s son yes yes
475   Unknown f 23 F s dau yes yes
476   Unknown m 21 F s son yes yes
477   Unknown f 19 F s dau yes yes

478   Na-he m 51 F m Head yes yes
479   Lucy f 59 F m wife yes yes

Florida Seminoles Indian Census (As of January 1, 1937)

KEY: Census Number Name Sex Age at Last Birthday Tribe (Seminole, unless otherwise stated) Degree of Blood Marital Status Relationship to Head of Family At Jurisdiction where enrolled [Yes or No] (If no, Where) Ward [Yes or No] Allotment, Annuity, and Identification Numbers (if given).

480   San-tee m 35 F s Head yes yes

481   Tiger m 42 F m Head yes yes
482   Ruby f 39 F m wife yes yes
483   Frank m 18 F s son yes yes
484   Cypress m 14 F s son yes yes
485   Harjo m 12 F s son yes yes
486   Unknown f 8 (2-18-28) F s dau yes yes
487   Unknown f 6 F s dau yes yes

488   Tiger Boy [Jimmie] m 22 F m Head yes yes
489   So-ko-yee [Martha] f 19 F m wife yes yes
490   Lum-hee m 1 (9-20-35) F s son yes yes

491   Willie m 67 F w Head yes yes

TIGERTAIL

492   John White m 22 F s Head yes yes
493   Unknown f 30 F w half-sis yes yes
494   Lena f 21 F s sister yes yes
495   Frances f 16 F s sister yes yes

496   Kat-ath-lee m 21 F s Head yes yes
497   Mable f 24 F w Head yes yes
498   Martha f 6 F s dau yes yes

TOMMIE

499   Annie f 81 F w Head yes yes
500   Annie Mae f 43 F s dau yes yes
501   Brownie m 38 F s son yes yes

502   Ben m 54 F m Head yes yes
503   Tudie f 42 F m wife yes yes
504   Mary f 15 (6-17-21) F s dau yes yes
505   **Tiger, Missie** f 49 F s sis-in-law yes yes
506   **Parker, Mary** f 14 (8-22-22) F s niece yes yes

149

Florida Seminoles Indian Census (As of January 1, 1937)

KEY: Census Number Name Sex Age at Last Birthday Tribe (Seminole, unless otherwise stated) Degree of Blood Marital Status Relationship to Head of Family At Jurisdiction where enrolled [Yes or No] (If no, Where) Ward [Yes or No] Allotment, Annuity, and Identification Numbers (if given).

507 **Parker, Agnes** f 12 (7-22-24) F s niece yes yes

508 Frank m 41 F m Head yes yes
509 Sadie f 31 F m wife yes yes
510 Willie Micco m 10 F s son yes yes
511 O-kay m 7 F s son yes yes
512 Hazel f 1 (11-23-35) F s dau yes yes   [Died 5-5-37]

513 Jack m 39 F m Head yes yes
514 Sally f 32 F m wife yes yes
515 Herbert Hoover m 19 F s son yes yes
516 George m 15 F s son yes yes
517 Fred Smith m 13 F s son yes yes
518 Rosa Lee f 12 F s dau yes yes
519 Odin m 10 F s son yes yes
520 Edward m 8 (8-12-28) F s son yes yes
521 Dick m 6 F s son yes yes
522 Minnie f 4 F s dau yes yes
523 Unknown f 2/12 (11-1-36) F s dau yes yes

524 Jim m, 41 F m Head yes yes
525 Lo-bee f 33 F m wife yes yes
526 Billie m 10 F s son yes yes
527 Jimmie m 7 F s son yes yes
528 As-sa-po-ha-tee f 4 (10-19-33) F s dau yes yes

529 Noki [Lady] f 33 F w Head yes yes
530 Baby Morgan f 12 F s dau yes yes

531 Sam m 32 F m Head yes yes
532 Mary f 23 F m wife yes yes
533 Harry m 6 F s son yes yes
534 Sadie f 4 (10-1-32) F s dau yes yes
535 Oct-sa-ta-kee f 6/12 (5-24-36) F s dau yes yes
536 Small-pox m 50 F m Head yes yes
537 Mary f 42 F m wife yes yes

Florida Seminoles Indian Census (As of January 1, 1937)

KEY: Census Number Name Sex Age at Last Birthday Tribe (Seminole, unless otherwise stated) Degree of Blood Marital Status Relationship to Head of Family At Jurisdiction where enrolled [Yes or No] (If no, Where) Ward [Yes or No] Allotment, Annuity, and Identification Numbers (if given).

TONY

538	Capt. Young m 55 F m Head yes yes
539	Unknown f 49 F m wife yes yes
540	Stim-pa-ha-hee f 24 F s dau yes yes
541	**Billie, Unknown** m 35 F s nephew yes yes
542	**Doctor, Jimmie Wilson** m 30 F s nephew yes yes
543	**Doctor, Unknown** f 32 F s niece yes yes

TUCKER

544	Chaw-huc-kee f 75 F w Head yes yes
545	Susie f 59 F s dau yes yes
546	Mait-kah f 56 F s dau yes yes
547	Sar-thler-na-kee f 33 F s dau yes yes
548	**Tiger, Willie** m 31 F s grnd-son yes yes
549	**Tiger, Flora** f 29 F s grnd-dau yes yes

550	Frank m 31 F m Head yes yes
551	Mary f 27 F m wife yes yes
552	Billie m 2 F s son yes yes
553	Unknown f 6/12 (5-7-36) F s dau yes yes

554	Oscar m 41 F m Head yes yes
555	Cotner f 38 F m wife yes yes
556	Cos-sum-lak-chee f 22 F s dau yes yes
557	Unknown m 19 F s son yes yes
558	Unknown m 16 f s son yes yes
559	Unknown m 13 F s son yes yes

WALKER

560	Henry m 69 F m Head yes yes
561	Unknown f 57 F m wife yes yes
562	Unknown f 33 f s dau yes yes

| 563 | Wat-cha-kee m 35 F s Head yes yes |

KEY: Census Number Name Sex Age at Last Birthday Tribe (Seminole, unless otherwise stated) Degree of Blood Marital Status Relationship to Head of Family At Jurisdiction where enrolled [Yes or No] (If no, Where) Ward [Yes or No] Allotment, Annuity, and Identification Numbers (if given).

WELLS

564   Ben m 28 F s Head yes yes

WILLIE

565   Frank m 52 F m Head yes yes
566   Ba-shee f 30 F m wife yes yes
567   O-mas-kee m 20 F s son yes yes
568   Yo-pote-ama f 18 F s dau yes yes
569   **Charlie, Pauline** f 11 F s stp-dau yes yes

570   Jessie m 37 F m Head yes yes
571   Unknown f 34 F m wife yes yes
572   Unknown f 17 F s dau yes yes
573   Unknown f 16 F s dau yes yes

574   Johnny m 67 F w Head yes yes

575   Sam m 45 F m Head yes yes
576   Unknown f 37 F m wife yes yes
577   Walter Roy m 15 F s son yes yes
578   Mary f 12 F s dau yes yes
579   Unknown m 10 F s son yes yes

580   Henry Sam m 18 F m Head yes yes
581   Mickie f 20 F m wife yes yes
582   Calvin m 4/12 (8-25-36) F s son yes yes

583   Sam Frank m 21 F m Head yes yes
584   Coh-co-me-ye f 21 F m wife yes yes
585   Unknown m 7 F s son yes yes
586   Unknown f 10/12 (2-13-36) F s dau yes yes

Florida Seminoles Indian Census (As of January 1, 1938)

KEY: 1937 Census Roll Number Last Census Roll Number of Head of Family Name Sex Date of Birth Tribe (Seminole, unless otherwise stated) Exact Degree of Blood Marital Status Relation to Head of Family At Jurisdiction where enrolled [Yes or No] (If no, Where) Ward [Yes or No]. (**NOTE:** "?" has been inserted where information was been left blank on original form.)

List only additions to 1937 Census Roll

64	63	Billie Edna	f	1918	F	s	niece	yes	
	548	Tiger, Maggie	?	1924	?	m	wife	?	
17	16	Billie, Peggy	f	1918	F	m	wife	yes	
	17	?	?	?	?	w	Head	?	
63	63	Billie, Rosalie	f	14	F	w	Head	yes	
	353	Osceola	?	?	?	m	wife	?	
25	23	Billie, Unknown	f	1927	F	s	dau	yes	
	75	Annie	?	1921	?	m	wife	?	
44	43	Billie, Unknown	f	1886	F	m	wife	yes	
	44	I-yoc-chee	?	?	?	w	Head	?	
77	76	Buster, Bessie	f	1925	½	s	dau	yes	
	289	Jumper	?	?	?	m	wife	?	
89	86	Bowers, Lydee	f	1912	F	s	stp-dau	yes	
	-----	Shore, Lottie	?	?	?	m	wife	?	
145	143	Cypress, Anna	f	1914	F	s	dau	yes	
	467	Tiger, Mary	?	?	?	m	wife	?	
146	143	Cypress, Betty Mae	f	1916	F	s	dau	yes	
	367	Osceola	?	?	?	m	wife	?	

153

Florida Seminoles Indian Census (As of January 1, 1938)

KEY: 1937 Census Roll Number Last Census Roll Number of Head of Family Name Sex Date of Birth Tribe (Seminole, unless otherwise stated) Exact Degree of Blood Marital Status Relation to Head of Family At Jurisdiction where enrolled [Yes or No] (If no, Where) Ward [Yes or No]. (**NOTE:** "?" has been inserted where information was been left blank on original form.)

124 124 Cypress, Mrs. Frank f 1916 F w Head yes

     16 Billie, Lucy Johns ? ? ? m wife ?

159 156 Dixie, Susie f 1910 ¾ w dau yes

   221 Jim ? ? ? m wife ?

203 203 Huff, Alice f 1916 F w Head yes
   372 Osceola ? ? ? m wife ?
216 212 Jim, Ah-po-kee f 1914 F s niece yes
   191 Frazier ? ? ? m wife ?

267 266 Johns, Maud f 1918 F s dau yes
   196 Gopher ? ? ? m wife ?

300 300 Jumper, Katy f 1905 F w Head yes

   425 Smith ? ? ? m wife ?

290 289 Jumper, Lena f 1911 F m wife yes
    65 Billie ? ? ? ? ? ?

307 306 Jumper, Stem-i-he-ooh f 1900 F s dau yes

   346 Osceola, Ar-she-yee ? 1893 ? m wife ?

347 346 Osceola, Lena f 1918 F s dau yes

   567 Frank ? ? ? m wife ?

348 346 Osceola, Mattie f 1920 F s dau yes

----- Doctor, Mary ? ? ? m wife ?
369 365 Osceola, Unknown f 1920 F s dau yes

Florida Seminoles Indian Census (As of January 1, 1938)

KEY: 1937 Census Roll Number Last Census Roll Number of Head of Family Name Sex Date of Birth Tribe (Seminole, unless otherwise stated) Exact Degree of Blood Marital Status Relation to Head of Family At Jurisdiction where enrolled [Yes or No] (If no, Where) Ward [Yes or No]. (**NOTE:** "?" has been inserted where information was been left blank on original form.)

313   Micco, Mina ? ? ? m wife ?

85   81   Pearce, Anna f 1913 ½ s niece yes

88   Bowers ? ? ? m wife ?

421 419   Smith, Ruby f 1917 F s dau yes

92   Bowers ? ? ? m wife ?

466 464   Tiger, Unknown f 1901 F s dau yes

43   Billie, Lucy ? ? ? m wife ?

468 464   Tiger, Unknown f 1908 F s dau yes

-----   Billie ? ? ? m wife ?

497 497   Tigertail, Mable f 1914 F w Head yes

-----   Billie ? ? ? m wife ?

Births (For 1938)

KEY: Last Census Roll Number of Head of Family Name Sex Date of Birth Tribe (Seminole, unless otherwise stated) Exact Degree of Blood Relation to Head of Family At Jurisdiction where enrolled [Yes or No] (If no, Where) County. [(If Died Before Enrollment - DBE, this will be noted at end of entry)].

13 Billie, Alva f 8-9-38 F dau yes Dade

55 Billie, Nanette f 10-19-38 F dau yes Collier

1 Billie, Silver Springs m 1-2-38 F son yes Marion

29 Billie, Unknown f 2-17-38 F dau yes Collier

88 Bowers, Unknown f 12-4-38 7/8 dau yes Glades

109 Buster Unknown f 7-8-38 F dau yes Glades

130 Cypress, Unknown f 7-26-38 F dau yes Hendry [DBE]

------ Doctor, Unknown f 3-10-38 F dau yes Dade

186 Fewell, Peggy f 11-7-38 F dau yes Broward

567 Frank, Unknown f 4-25-38 F dau yes Dade

206 Huff, Agnes f 10-20-38 F dau yes Glades

220 Jim, Mary Jean f 12-31-38 F s niece yes Dade

296 Jumper, Ma-tha-cha-chee f 9-23-38 F dau yes Glades

313 Micco, Unknown f 2-8-38 F dau yes Hendry

328 Motloe, Ella f 5-3-38 f dau yes Collier

372 Osceola, Bobby m 3-11-38 F son yes Glades

389 Osceola, Juanita f 8-27-38 F dau yes Martin

356 Osceola, Unknown f 1-?-38 F dau yes Collier

375 Osceola, Unknown f 9-13-38 F dau yes Dade

Births (For 1938)

KEY: Last Census Roll Number of Head of Family Name Sex Date of Birth Tribe (Seminole, unless otherwise stated) Exact Degree of Blood Relation to Head of Family At Jurisdiction where enrolled [Yes or No] (If no, Where) County. [(If Died Before Enrollment - DBE, this will be noted at end of entry)].

395   Osceola, Unknown f 1-17-38 F dau yes Dade

------   Shore, Unknown m 6-2-38 F son yes Glades   [DBE]

423   Smith, Unknown m 7-11-39 F son yes Glades   [DBE]

544   Tiger, Unknown f 3-9-38 F great grnd-dau yes Glades

548   Tiger, Unknown f 12-31-38 F dau yes Collier

524   Tommie, Nok-co-chee f 8-2-38 F dau yes Dade

531   Tommie, Sa-wa-hee m 5-29-38 F son yes Palm Beach

550   Tucker, A-no-ki m 9-12-38 F son yes Dade

580   Willie, Unknown m 6-30-38 F son yes Dade

Deaths (Between January 1, 1936, and December 31, 1938)

KEY: Census Number and Year (If Died Before Enrollment, DBE will be inserted) Name Death Date Age at Death Sex Tribe (Seminole, unless otherwise stated) Ward [Yes or No] Degree of Blood Cause of Death At Jurisdiction where enrolled [Yes or No] (If no, Where).

26 1934 Billie, John 7-16-36 91 m yes F Dysentery yes

153 1934 Billie, Mrs. Miami 9-13-36 101 f yes F Influenza yes

54 1934 Billie, Minnie 8-14-36 12 f yes F Chronic Epilepsy yes

DBE Billie, Unknown 9-30-36 4 da f yes F Unknown yes

DBE Billie Unknown 9-27-36 2 hr m yes F Premature yes

DBE Billie, Unknown 9-27-36 2 hr f yes F Premature yes

103 1934 Buster, Mis-tee 11-1-36 56 f yes F Unknown yes

DBE Johns Rosa 6-13-36 5½ f yes ½ Indian & ½ White Acute Dilatation of Heart yes

DBE Smith, Sampson 3-25-36 15 m yes 7/8 Indian & 1/8 Negro Drowned in canal yes

498 1934 Tigertail, Edna 1-15-36 22 f yes F Drowned in canal yes

496 1934 Tigertail, Wilson 12-7-36 26 m yes F Run over by car on Trail yes

(January 1 thru December 31, 1938)

31 1938 Billie, John 11-15-38 45 m yes F Unknown yes

39 1937 Billie, John P 2-24-38 28 m yes F Gun shot wound yes

DBE Cypress, Unknown 7-28-38 2da f yes F Unknown yes

248 1937 Johns, Annie 1-9-38 65 f yes F Pneumonia yes

DBE Shore, Unknown 6-2-38 6 hr m yes F Unknown yes

Deaths (Between January 1, 1936, and December 31, 1938)

KEY: Census Number and Year (If Died Before Enrollment, DBE will be inserted) Name Death Date Age at Death Sex Tribe (Seminole, unless otherwise stated) Ward [Yes or No] Degree of Blood Cause of Death At Jurisdiction where enrolled [Yes or No] (If no, Where).

DBE   Smith, Unknown 7-16-38 5 da m yes F Unknown yes

505   1937   Tiger, Missie 12-19-38 50 f yes F Acute dehydration accidosis yes

538   1937   Tony, Capt. Young 8-20-38 57 m yes F Appendicile abscess yes

17   1938   Willie, Unknown 7-27-38 9/12 f yes F Unknown yes

UNREPORTED DEATHS
(January 1 thru December 31, 1933)

68   1934   Billie, Unknown 1933 6 m yes F Unknown yes

(January 1 thru December 31, 1935)

322   1934   Smith, Billie 1935 4 m yes F Unknown yes

(January 1 thru December 31, 1937)

19   1937   Billie, George 11-20-37 19 m yes F Unknown yes

106   1937   Buster, Nellie 6-5-37 86 f yes F Unknown yes

135   1937   Cypress, Gene Sterling 2-28-37 1 m yes F Dysentery yes

219   1937   Jim, Wa-ti-kee 6-22-37 65 f yes F Blood infection yes

336   1937   Motloe, Billie 1-15-37 81 m yes F Dropsy yes

DBE   Osceola, Unknown 12-17-37 4 da m yes F Improper care yes

464   1937   Tiger, Jim 6-8-37 55 m yes F Pneumonia yes

463   1937   Tiger, Mrs. Jim 9-17-37 65 f yes F Drowned yes

Deaths (Between January 1, 1936, and December 31, 1938)

KEY: Census Number and Year (If Died Before Enrollment, DBE will be inserted) Name Death Date Age at Death Sex Tribe (Seminole, unless otherwise stated) Ward [Yes or No] Degree of Blood Cause of Death At Jurisdiction where enrolled [Yes or No] (If no, Where).

469   1937   Tiger, Unknown 9-17-37 25 f yes F Drowned yes

512   1937   Tommie, Hazel 5-5-37 1 f yes F Pneumonia yes

Florida Seminoles Indian Census (As of January 1, 1940)

KEY: Family's Resident County, (State of Florida, unless otherwise stated) Census Number Name Sex Age at Last Birthday Tribe (Seminole, unless otherwise stated) Degree of Blood Marital Status Relationship to Head of Family At Jurisdiction where enrolled [Yes or No] (If no, Where) Resident County (State of Florida, unless otherwise stated) Ward [Yes or No].

BILLIE

Hendry Co.
1   Albert m 40 F m Head yes yes
2   Willie f 38 F m wife yes yes
3   Marian f 9 (5-5-30) F s dau yes yes
4   Silver Springs m 1 (1-2-38) F s son yes yes

Collier Co.
5   Alice f 21 F w Head yes yes
6   Mary f 6 F s dau yes yes
7   Unknown f 1 (2-17-38) F s dau yes yes

Collier Co.
8   Annie f 20 F w Head yes yes
9   Harvey m 2 (5-7-37) F s son yes yes
10   John m 2/12 (10-5-39) F s son yes yes

Hendry Co.
11   (Boy), Charlie m 24 F m Head yes yes
12   Annie f 37 F m wife yes yes
13   Frances Stearns f 3 (1-5-36) F s dau yes yes
14   **Doctor, Jimmie** m 15 F s stp-son yes yes
15   **Doctor, Billie** m 10 F s stp-son yes yes

Collier Co.
16   Chestnut m 34 F m Head yes yes
17   To-li-kee [Betty] f 27 F m wife yes yes
18   Alva f 1 (8-9-38) F s dau yes yes

Dade Co.
19   Cowboy m 30 F w Head yes yes

Hendry Co.
20   Frank m 26 F m Head yes yes
21   Lucy John f 25 (12-?-14) F m wife yes yes
22   **Cypress, Herbert Mills** m 6 (9-30-33) F s stp-son yes yes

Florida Seminoles Indian Census (As of January 1, 1940)

KEY: **Family's Resident County**, (State of Florida, unless otherwise stated) Census Number Name Sex Age at Last Birthday Tribe (Seminole, unless otherwise stated) Degree of Blood Marital Status Relationship to Head of Family At Jurisdiction where enrolled [Yes or No] (If no, Where) Resident County (State of Florida, unless otherwise stated) Ward [Yes or No].

Collier Co.
23   Homespun m 49 F s Head yes yes

Collier Co.
24   Ingram m 50 F m Head yes yes
25   Is-tem-e-thee f 44 F m wife yes yes
26   Thee-lo-kee [Effie] m 9 F s son yes yes

Collier Co.
27   I-yoc-chee f 34 F w Head yes yes

Glades Co.
28   Jack m 20 F m Head yes yes
29   Lena Huff f 30 F m wife yes yes
30   A-lee-san-ta [Mary] f 5/12 (6-29-39) F s dau yes yes
31   **Jumper, Lois** f 6 (9-26-33) F s stp-dau yes yes
32   **Jumper, Billie** m 4 (6-28-35) F s stp-son yes yes

Collier Co.
33   Jimmie m 39 F m Head yes yes
34   Oc-o-tee f 34 F m wife yes yes
35   Fic-ho-wa-mee f 6 F s dau yes yes
36   Unknown m 4 F s son yes yes

Hendry Co.
37   Jimmie m 27 F m Head yes yes
38   Josie f 17 F m wife yes yes

Hendry Co.
39   Jimmie Girtman m 26 F s Head yes yes

Collier Co.
40   John m 36 F m Head yes
41   Lena f 31 F m wife yes yes

Glades Co.
42   John m 34 F w Head yes yes
43   Homer m 11 F s son yes yes

KEY: Family's Resident County, (State of Florida, unless otherwise stated) Census Number
Name Sex Age at Last Birthday Tribe (Seminole, unless otherwise stated) Degree of Blood
Marital Status Relationship to Head of Family At Jurisdiction where enrolled [Yes or No] (If no,
Where) Resident County (State of Florida, unless otherwise stated) Ward [Yes or No].

44   Maxie m 7 (12-24-32) F s son yes yes

Dade Co.
45   Johnny m 19 f s Head yes yes
46   Larry m 14 F s brother yes yes
47   Minnie f 13 F s sister yes yes
48   Peggy f 9 F s sister yes yes

Collier Co.
49   Josie m 52 (12-12-87) F m Head yes yes
50   Lucy Tiger f 39 F m wife yes yes

Glades Co.
51   Julia f 35 F w Head yes yes
52   **Smith, Louise** f 10 F s dau yes yes
53   **Smith, Jim Stewart** m 7 (10-18-32) F s son yes yes

Collier Co.
54   Con-cho [Kunzie] m 46 F m Head yes yes
55   Addie f 41 F m wife yes yes
56   Unknown m 13 F s son yes yes
57   Unknown m 10 F s son yes yes
58   Unknown m 4 F s son yes yes

Hendry Co.
59   Little Charlie m 43 F m Head yes yes
60   He-sha-wee f 58 F m wife yes yes

Collier Co.
61   Wat-see [Louise] f 50 F w Head yes yes
62   Effie f 20 F s dau yes yes
63   Frances f 15 (1924) F s dau yes yes
64   Paul m 12 (1927) F s son yes yes

Hendry Co.
65   Lo-ke-pee m 15 F s Head yes yes
66   We-he-lee m 13 F s brother yes yes
67   O-me-chee m 11 F s brother yes yes

Florida Seminoles Indian Census (As of January 1, 1940)

KEY: Family's Resident County, (State of Florida, unless otherwise stated) Census Number Name Sex Age at Last Birthday Tribe (Seminole, unless otherwise stated) Degree of Blood Marital Status Relationship to Head of Family At Jurisdiction where enrolled [Yes or No] (If no, Where) Resident County (State of Florida, unless otherwise stated) Ward [Yes or No].

68   So-pa-hi-mee f 8 F s sister yes yes

Glades Co.
69   Mabel f 24 F w Head yes yes
70   Rosie f 2 (10-26-37) F s dau yes yes

Collier Co.
71   Old Charlie m 59 F m Head yes yes
72   Mona f 60 F m wife yes yes
73   Maggie f 28 F s dau yes yes
------ Ollie f 13 F s ? yes yes   [See #346]

Dade Co.
74   Peggy f 22 F w Head yes yes
75   Ho-lee-chi-chee f 5 (8-2-34) F s dau yes yes

Collier Co.
76   Robert m 38 F m Head yes yes
77   Josie f 33 F m wife yes yes
78   Milton m 10 F s son yes yes
79   Weaver m 7 (12-25-32) F s son yes yes
80   Nanette f 1 (10-19-38) F s dau yes yes

Collier Co.
81   Romeo [Johnson] m 32 F m Head yes yes
82   Annie f 24 F m wife yes yes
83   Charlie m 7 F s son yes yes
84   Jimmie m 5 F s son yes yes
85   Unknown m ? (12-8-39) F s son yes yes

Collier Co.
86   That-kee f 32 F w Head yes yes
87   Unknown m 11/12 (1-30-39) F s son yes yes

Dade Co.
88   Tommie f 31 F w Head yes yes
89   Effie f 14 F s dau yes yes
90   Agnes f 12 F s dau yes yes

Florida Seminoles Indian Census (As of January 1, 1940)

KEY: Family's Resident County, (State of Florida, unless otherwise stated) Census Number Name Sex Age at Last Birthday Tribe (Seminole, unless otherwise stated) Degree of Blood Marital Status Relationship to Head of Family At Jurisdiction where enrolled [Yes or No] (If no, Where) Resident County (State of Florida, unless otherwise stated) Ward [Yes or No].

Glades Co.
91   Watts m 21 F m Head yes yes
92   Mabel f 26 F m wife yes yes
93   **Tigertail, Frances** f 9 F s stp-dau yes yes

Glades Co.
94   Willie m 50 F w Head yes yes

BIGLOW

Glades Co.
------ Mamie f 35 F w ? yes yes [See 359]
------ Lauderdale f 7 (12-1-32) F s ? yes yes [See 340]

BOWERS

Glades Co.
95   Andrew Jackson m 28 F m Head yes yes
96   Anna Pearce f 27 ¾ m wife yes yes
97   Unknown f 1 (12-3-38) 7/8 s dau yes yes

Hendry Co.
98   Dick m 24 F m Head yes yes
99   Marian f 23 F m wife yes yes

Glades Co.
------ Joe m 18 F s ? yes yes [See 112]
------ Casey m 16 F s ? yes yes [See 113]

Collier Co.
100   Lillie Stone f 38 F w Head yes yes
101   Elizabeth f 9 F s dau yes yes
102   **Willie, Ruby** f 49 F w sister yes yes
103   **Willie, Little** m 10 (1-15-29) F s nephew yes yes

Glades Co.
104   Tom m 20 F m Head yes yes
105   Ruby Smith f 23 F m wife yes yes

165

Florida Seminoles Indian Census (As of January 1, 1940)

KEY: Family's Resident County, (State of Florida, unless otherwise stated) Census Number Name Sex Age at Last Birthday Tribe (Seminole, unless otherwise stated) Degree of Blood Marital Status Relationship to Head of Family At Jurisdiction where enrolled [Yes or No] (If no, Where) Resident County (State of Florida, unless otherwise stated) Ward [Yes or No].

BOWLEGS

Glades Co.
106   Billie m 73 ½ w Head yes yes
107   **Tucker, Lewis** m 51 ½ s bro yes yes
108   **Pearce, Lucy** f 58 ½ w sis yes yes
109   **Pearce, Ada** f 29 ¾ s niece yes yes

Glades Co.
110   Eli Morgan m 44 ¾ m Head yes yes
111   Lena Doctor f 40 F m wife yes yes
112   **Bowers, Joe** m 18 F s stp-son yes yes
113   **Bowers, Casey** m 16 F s stp-son yes yes

BUCK

Collier Co.
114   John m 42 F w Head yes yes

BUSTER

Hendry Co.
115   Billie m 95 F w Head yes yes

Hendry Co.
116   Billie m 34 F s Head yes yes

Glades Co.
117   Charlie m 68 F w Head yes yes

St. Lucie Co.
118   Annie f 43 F s Head yes yes
119   Yek-am-kah f 41 F s sister yes yes

Hendry Co.
120   Johnny m 50 F m Head yes yes
121   In-git-ta-hi-yee f 52 F m wife yes yes
122   Junior m 13 F s son yes yes

Florida Seminoles Indian Census (As of January 1, 1940)

KEY: **Family's Resident County**, (State of Florida, unless otherwise stated) Census Number Name Sex Age at Last Birthday Tribe (Seminole, unless otherwise stated) Degree of Blood Marital Status Relationship to Head of Family At Jurisdiction where enrolled [Yes or No] (If no, Where) Resident County (State of Florida, unless otherwise stated) Ward [Yes or No].

123   Se-ne-hee f 11 F s dau yes yes

Hendry Co.
124   Lucy f 33 F s Head yes yes

Glades Co.
125   Tom m 21 F m Head yes yes
126   Ruby f 22 F m wife yes yes
127   A-dish-ma-ha f 1 (7-8-38) F s dau yes yes

CHARLIE

Glades Co.
------ Big m 57 F s ? yes yes [See 459]

Collier Co.
128   Frank m 29 f m Head yes yes
129   Carrie f 28 F m wife yes yes
Dade Co.
------ Pauline f 21 F s ? yes yes [See 566]

CLAY

Collier Co.
130   Mrs. Henry f 50 F w Head yes yes
131   Abraham Lincoln m 45 F s stp-son yes yes
132   Lula f 23 F s dau yes yes
133   Henry m 20 F s son yes yes

Hendry Co.
134   Jack [Johnson] m 36 F m Head yes yes
135   Ruby f 32 F m wife yes yes
136   Bob m 4 (3-28-35) F s son yes yes

CYPRESS

Hendry Co.
137   Charlie m 71 F m Head yes yes

Florida Seminoles Indian Census (As of January 1, 1940)

138   Lee Billie f 56 F m wife yes yes
139   Ada f 16 F s dau yes yes
140   Stanley Hanson m 12 F s son yes yes

Collier Co.
141   Futch m 64 F m Head yes yes
142   A-ah-fo-ke-lut-kee f 53 F m wife yes yes
143   Shin-tats-poy-chee [Bert] m 16 F s son yes yes
144   O-hi-yio-chee m 14 F s son yes yes

Hendry Co.
145   Henry m 35 F w Head yes yes

Hendry Co.
------   Herbert Mills m 6 (9-30-33) F s ? yes yes   [See 22]

Hendry Co.
146   John m 38 F m Head yes yes
147   Me-tha-ha-yee f 18 F m wife yes yes
148   Na-ti-he-yee m 6/12 (5-20-39) F s son yes yes

Hendry Co.
149   Mary [Mrs. John] f 33 F w Head yes yes
150   Stanee Hansee m 12 (12-18-27) F s son yes yes
151   Buck m 9 (5-1-30) F s son yes yes
152   Julia Graves f 6 (5-23-33) F s dau yes yes

Hendry Co.
153   Little m 33 F m Head yes yes
154   Mary f 25 F m wife yes yes
155   Sa-tha-ma-hee m 6 (5-6-33) F s son yes yes
156   Etta f 5 (10-20-34) F s dau yes yes
157   Minnie f 3 (1936) F s dau yes yes

Collier Co.
------   Mary Jean f 7 F s ? yes yes   [See 556]

Florida Seminoles Indian Census (As of January 1, 1940)

KEY: **Family's Resident County**, (State of Florida, unless otherwise stated) Census Number Name Sex Age at Last Birthday Tribe (Seminole, unless otherwise stated) Degree of Blood Marital Status Relationship to Head of Family At Jurisdiction where enrolled [Yes or No] (If no, Where) Resident County (State of Florida, unless otherwise stated) Ward [Yes or No].

Hendry Co.
158   Whitney m 65 F m Head yes yes
159   Sally f 66 F m wife yes yes
160   Junior m 21 F s son yes yes
161   Mary f 18 (10-2-21) F s dau yes yes
162   Jimmie m 16 F s son yes yes

Hendry Co.
163   Wilson m 63 F m Head yes yes
164   Ruby f 46 F m wife yes yes
165   Lena f 24 F s dau yes yes
166   Salle f 22 F s dau yes yes
167   Frank m 17 F s son yes yes
168   Ke-ya-he-yee [Tony] m 5 F s grnd-son yes yes

DIXIE

Hendry Co.
169   Charlie m 73 ½ w Head yes yes
170   Walter Huff m 34 ¾ s son yes yes
171   Sampson m 17 ¾ s son yes yes

Hendry Co.
------ Dodie m 6 (7-15-33) 7/8 s ? yes yes   [See 237]

DOCTOR

Collier Co.
172   Harry m 45 F m Head yes yes
173   Annie f 52 F m wife yes yes
174   Pa-mo-kee f 22 F s dau yes yes
175   Mos-kee f 21 F s dau yes yes
176   Is-tan-e-hic-chee f 20 F s dau yes yes
177   Shee-poc-e-nee-kee m 13 F s son yes yes
178   Unknown m 8 F s son yes yes
179   Unknown f 6 F s dau yes yes

Florida Seminoles Indian Census (As of January 1, 1940)

KEY: **Family's Resident County**, (State of Florida, unless otherwise stated) Census Number Name Sex Age at Last Birthday Tribe (Seminole, unless otherwise stated) Degree of Blood Marital Status Relationship to Head of Family At Jurisdiction where enrolled [Yes or No] (If no, Where) Resident County (State of Florida, unless otherwise stated) Ward [Yes or No].

Collier Co.
180   Jim Henry m 21 F m Head yes yes
181   Mattie f 20 F m wife yes yes
182   Bobbie m 2 (2-8-37) F s son yes yes

Hendry Co.
------   Jimmie m 15 F s ? yes yes
------   Billie m 10 F s ? yes yes

Collier Co.
183   Joe m 22 F m Head yes yes
184   Mary f 20 F m wife yes yes
185   Nellie f 1 (3-10-38) F s dau yes yes

Hendry Co.
186   Little m 54 F m Head yes yes
187   Mamie f 43 F m wife yes yes
188   Ka-ni-kee f 20 F s dau yes yes
189   Al-wee f 17 F s dau yes yes

Collier Co.
190   Wilson m 40 F m Head yes yes
191   O-sa-fe-chee f 36 F m wife yes yes
192   Jimmie m 10 F s son yes yes
193   Is-tin-go-wi-chee m 6 (6-6-33) F s son yes yes
194   Lol-ley m 2 (1937) F s son yes yes
195   Unknown f 5/12 (7-20-39) F s dau yes yes

FEWELL

Collier Co.
196   Charlie m 73 F m Head yes yes
197   Cha-kee f 73 F m wife yes yes
198   Little m 21 F s son yes yes
199   Maggie f 18 F s dau yes yes

Broward Co.
200   Eula f 36 F w Head yes yes

KEY: **Family's Resident County**, (State of Florida, unless otherwise stated) Census Number Name Sex Age at Last Birthday Tribe (Seminole, unless otherwise stated) Degree of Blood Marital Status Relationship to Head of Family At Jurisdiction where enrolled [Yes or No] (If no, Where) Resident County (State of Florida, unless otherwise stated) Ward [Yes or No].

201   Juanita f 15 F s dau yes yes
202   Martha f 3 (3-26-36) F s dau yes yes
203   Peggy f 1 (11-7-38) F s dau yes yes

Glades Co.
204   Johnny m 40 F m Head yes yes
205   Mary f 44 F m wife yes yes

FRANK

Dade Co.
206   Sam m 27 F m Head yes yes
207   Unknown f 21 F m wife yes yes
208   Win-na-hee f 8 F s dau yes yes
209   Ta-chee f 6 F s dau yes yes
210   Ho-la-chee m 2 (6-?-37) F s son yes yes

Dade Co.
211   Willie m 23 F m Head yes yes
212   Lena f 22 F m wife yes yes
213   Ethel f 1 (4-25-38) F s dau yes yes

FRAZIER

Collier Co.
214   Byrd m 42 F m Head yes yes
215   Ah-po-kee f 26 F m wife yes yes
216   **Jim, Unknown** m 11 F s stp-son yes yes

Collier Co.
------   John Bird m 13 F s ? yes yes [See 378]
------   Henry Byrd m 10 F s ? yes yes [See 379]

GOPHER

Broward Co.
217   Jim m 70 F w Head yes yes
218   Ada f 41 F s dau yes yes

Florida Seminoles Indian Census (As of January 1, 1940)

KEY: Family's Resident County, (State of Florida, unless otherwise stated) Census Number Name Sex Age at Last Birthday Tribe (Seminole, unless otherwise stated) Degree of Blood Marital Status Relationship to Head of Family At Jurisdiction where enrolled [Yes or No] (If no, Where) Resident County (State of Florida, unless otherwise stated) Ward [Yes or No].

Glades Co.

219   John Henry m 24 F m Head yes yes
220   Maud Johns f 22 F m wife yes yes
221   John Sharp m 4/12 (8-22-39) F s son yes yes

Glades Co.

222   Lucy Tiger f 57 F w Head yes yes
223   Willie m 27 F s son yes yes
224   Annie f 23 F s dau yes yes
225   Lena f 22 F s dau yes yes
226   Unknown f 2 (10-11-37) F s grnd-dau yes yes

HUFF

Glades Co.

227   Frank m 27 F m Head yes yes
228   Mary f 31 F m wife yes yes
229   Holi-a-sho-bee [Stanley] m 2 (5-24-37) F s son yes yes
230   Agnes f 1 (10-20-38) F s dau yes yes

Glades Co.

------   George m 11 (11-8-28) F s ? yes yes

Glades Co.

------   Leoda f 7 (9-3-32) F s ? yes yes
------   Frances f 4 (7-16-35) F s ? yes yes

Glades Co.

231   Sam m 57 F w Head yes yes

JIM

Hendry Co.

232   Boy m 38 F s Head yes yes
233   Lola f 21 F s sister yes yes
234   Mary Jean f 1 (12-31-38) F s niece yes yes

172

Florida Seminoles Indian Census (As of January 1, 1940)

KEY: Family's Resident County, (State of Florida, unless otherwise stated) Census Number Name Sex Age at Last Birthday Tribe (Seminole, unless otherwise stated) Degree of Blood Marital Status Relationship to Head of Family At Jurisdiction where enrolled [Yes or No] (If no, Where) Resident County (State of Florida, unless otherwise stated) Ward [Yes or No].

Hendry Co.
235 Buffalo m 35 F m Head yes yes
236 Susie Dixie f 30 ¾ m wife yes yes
237 **Dixie, Dodie** m 6 (7-15-33) 7/8 s stp-son yes yes

Collier Co.
238 Frank m 40 F m Head yes yes
239 Annie f 27 F m wife yes yes
240 Unknown f 4 (3-16-35) F s dau yes yes
241 Unknown m 2 (3-12-37) F s son yes yes

Collier Co.
242 Henry m 50 F w Head yes yes

Collier Co.
243 Johnnie m 46 F w Head yes yes

Glades Co.
------ Little John m 21 F s ? yes yes [See 425]

Collier Co.
------ Unknown m 11 F s ? yes yes [See 216]

Collier Co.
244 Willie m 48 F m Head yes yes
245 Fo-le-chic-chee f 36 F m wife yes yes
246 Johnnie m 21 F s son yes yes
247 Jack m 19 F s son yes yes
248 Margurette f 17 F s dau yes yes
249 Pa-to-hee f 14 F s dau yes yes
250 Me-lo-hee-yee f 12 F s dau yes yes
251 Jimmie m 9 F s son yes yes
252 Unknown f 3 (12-1-36) F s dau yes yes

Dade Co.
253 Willie m 42 F m Head yes yes
254 Hic-ar-he-thee f 29 F m wife yes yes
255 Thelma f 19 F s dau yes yes

KEY: Family's Resident County, (State of Florida, unless otherwise stated) Census Number Name Sex Age at Last Birthday Tribe (Seminole, unless otherwise stated) Degree of Blood Marital Status Relationship to Head of Family At Jurisdiction where enrolled [Yes or No] (If no, Where) Resident County (State of Florida, unless otherwise stated) Ward [Yes or No].

256   Agnes f 16 F s dau yes yes
257   Mo-lo-yee f 14 F s dau yes yes
258   Billie m 6 F s son yes yes
259   Lewrence m 6/12 (6-14-39) ½ s grnd-son yes yes

JOHN

Hendry Co.
260   Bouton m 21 F m Head yes yes
261   Charlotte f 22 F m wife yes yes
262   Margarette f 8/12 (5-1-39) F s dau yes yes

Hendry Co.
------   Doctor m 51 F w ? yes yes
------   Jimmie f 17 F s ? yes yes

JOHNS

Glades Co.
263   Barfield m 26 F m Head yes yes
264   ? f 22 F m wife yes yes
265   Archie m 3 (7-24-36) F s son yes yes
266   Unknown f 2 (10-22-37) F s dau yes yes

Glades Co.
267   Dolly f 41 F s Head yes yes
268   Oscar m 38 F s brother yes yes
269   Arnie f 34 F s sister yes yes
270   Lizzie f 32 F s sister yes yes
271   Emma f 28 F s sister yes yes
272   Loy [Lillie] f 24 F s sister yes yes
273   Louise f 21 F s sister yes yes
274   Lena f 18 F s sister yes yes
275   Lottie f 8 ½ s niece yes yes
276   Wonder m 5 (5-28-34) ½ s nephew yes yes
277   Frankie m 4 (7-7-35) F s nephew yes yes

Florida Seminoles Indian Census (As of January 1, 1940)

KEY: **Family's Resident County**, (State of Florida, unless otherwise stated) Census Number Name Sex Age at Last Birthday Tribe (Seminole, unless otherwise stated) Degree of Blood Marital Status Relationship to Head of Family At Jurisdiction where enrolled [Yes or No] (If no, Where) Resident County (State of Florida, unless otherwise stated) Ward [Yes or No].

Glades Co.
278   Ernie f 52 F s Head yes yes

Glades Co.
279   Sheela Hilliard f 42 F w Head yes yes
280   Joe m 19 F s son yes yes

Glades Co.
281   Tobie m 30 F m Head yes yes
282   Rosa f 27 F m wife yes yes
283   Cecil m 4 F s son yes yes
284   Unknown f 2 (5-29-37) F s dau yes yes

JONES

St. Lucie Co.
285   Sam m 46 F m Head yes yes
286   Missie Stick f 44 F m wife yes yes
287   Feet f 26 F s dau yes yes
288   Willie Henry m 23 F s son yes yes
289   Doctor m 20 F s son yes yes
290   Annie f 18 F s dau yes yes
291   Arleta f 16 F s dau yes yes
292   Hot-to-gar f 14 F s dau yes yes
293   Sem-o-gar f 12 F s dau yes yes
294   Arlene m 10 F s son yes yes
295   Doctor Hill m 7 (5-1-32) F s son yes yes

JOSH

Glades Co.
296   John m 30 ¾ m Head yes yes
297   Henley Dennie f 33 F m wife yes yes
298   Shin-ta-ti-kee m 2 (8-5-37) 7/8 s son yes yes
299   -Fi-kee f 47 ½ w mother yes yes

175

Florida Seminoles Indian Census (As of January 1, 1940)

KEY: **Family's Resident County**, (State of Florida, unless otherwise stated) Census Number Name Sex Age at Last Birthday Tribe (Seminole, unless otherwise stated) Degree of Blood Marital Status Relationship to Head of Family At Jurisdiction where enrolled [Yes or No] (If no, Where) Resident County (State of Florida, unless otherwise stated) Ward [Yes or No].

JUMPER

Collier Co.
300   Chief Charlie m 36 F m Head yes yes
301   Rosa Johns f 22 F m wife yes yes

Collier Co.
302   Harry m 29 F m Head yes yes
303   Tommie f 31 F m wife yes yes
304   Joe m 7 (6-2-32) F s son yes yes
305   Mary f 4 (8-20-35) F s dau yes yes
306   Unknown m 2 (9-?-37) F s son yes yes

Glades Co.
307   John m 30 F m Head yes yes
308   Bessie Buster f 16 ½ m wife yes yes

Collier Co.
309   Johnny m 53 F m Head yes yes
310   Kap-pe-thee f 60 F m wife yes yes

Glades Co.
311   Josie m 35 F m Head yes yes
312   Pocahontas f 30 F m wife yes yes
313   Allison Stanford m 3 (4-19-36) F s son yes yes
314   Unknown f 1 (9-23-38) F s dau yes yes
315   **Huff, George** m 11 (11-8-28) F s stp-son yes yes

Collier Co.
316   Little Charlie m 58 F m Head yes yes
317   Sally f 49 F m wife yes yes
318   Henry m 18 F s son yes yes

Glades Co.
------   Lois f 6 (9-26-33) F s ? yes yes [See 31]
------   Billie m 4 (6-28-35) F s ? yes yes [See 32]

Florida Seminoles Indian Census (As of January 1, 1940)

KEY: Family's Resident County, (State of Florida, unless otherwise stated) Census Number
Name Sex Age at Last Birthday Tribe (Seminole, unless otherwise stated) Degree of Blood
Marital Status Relationship to Head of Family At Jurisdiction where enrolled [Yes or No] (If no,
Where) Resident County (State of Florida, unless otherwise stated) Ward [Yes or No].

Glades Co.
------ Mosas m 13 (4-15-26) F s ? yes yes [See 439]
------ Lura f 8 (11-13-31) F s ? yes yes [See 440]

Glades Co.
319 Rosalie f 46 F w Head yes yes

Glades Co.
320 Mrs. Squirrel f 60 F w Head yes yes

Broward Co.
321 Willie m 70 F s Head yes yes

MICCO

Glades Co.
322 Charlie m 58 F m Head yes yes
323 Emma f 40 F m wife yes yes
324 Codie f 19 F s dau yes yes
325 Alice Lewis f 16 F s dau yes yes
326 Little Jack m 10 (8-1-29) F s son yes yes
327 Howard m 6 (7-23-33) F s son yes yes

Hendry Co.
328 Little Charlie m 24 F m Head yes yes
329 Mina Osceola f 20 F m wife yes yes
330 Unknown f 1 (2-28-38) F s dau yes yes

St. Lucie Co.
331 Oscar m 43 F m Head yes yes
332 Goodna f 40 F m wife yes yes
333 Homer f 22 F s dau yes yes
334 Dolly Whidden f 20 F s dau yes yes
335 Charlotte f 18 F s dau yes yes
336 In-no-gee f 16 F s dau yes yes
337 Lungo m 14 F s son yes yes

177

Florida Seminoles Indian Census (As of January 1, 1940)

KEY: **Family's Resident County**, (State of Florida, unless otherwise stated) Census Number Name Sex Age at Last Birthday Tribe (Seminole, unless otherwise stated) Degree of Blood Marital Status Relationship to Head of Family At Jurisdiction where enrolled [Yes or No] (If no, Where) Resident County (State of Florida, unless otherwise stated) Ward [Yes or No].

MORGAN

Glades Co.
338   Jake m 45 F w Head yes yes
339   **Biglow, Mamie** f 35 F w sister yes yes
340   **Biglow, Lauderdale** f 7 (12-1-32) F s niece yes yes

MOTLOE

Collier Co.
341   Jack m 46 F m Head yes yes
342   Belle Billie f 44 F m wife yes yes
343   Louise f 7 (12-2-32) F s dau yes yes
344   Mary f 3 (1-4-36) F s dau yes yes
345   Ella f 1 (5-3-38) F s dau yes yes
346   **Billie, Ollie** f 13 F s stp-dau yes yes

Collier Co.
347   John m 40 F m Head yes yes
348   La-shec-chee f 27 F m wife yes yes

OSCEOLA

Hendry Co.
349   Billie m 48 F m Head yes yes
350   Ar-she-yee f 46 F m wife yes yes
351   Jimmie m 13 F s son yes yes
352   **John, Doctor** m 51 F w bro-in-law yes yes
353   **John, Jimmie** f 17 F s niece yes yes

Collier Co.
354   Billie m 21 F m Head yes yes
355   Annie f 20 F m wife yes yes
356   **Cypress, Mary Jean** f 7 F s stp-dau yes yes

Glades Co.
357   Charlie m 33 F m Head yes yes
358   Rosalie f 26 F m wife yes yes

Florida Seminoles Indian Census (As of January 1, 1940)

KEY: **Family's Resident County**, (State of Florida, unless otherwise stated) Census Number Name Sex Age at Last Birthday Tribe (Seminole, unless otherwise stated) Degree of Blood Marital Status Relationship to Head of Family At Jurisdiction where enrolled [Yes or No] (If no, Where) Resident County (State of Florida, unless otherwise stated) Ward [Yes or No].

359   We-ha-ha-yee m 13 F s son yes yes
360   Ka-no-fo-lot-kee f 17 F s dau yes yes

Collier Co.
361   Cori m 34 F m Head yes yes
362   Juanita f 31 F m wife yes yes
363   Och-te-hi-kee f 12 (8-29-27) F s dau yes yes
364   Ar-ye-cha-shee m 9 F s son yes yes
365   Pattie m 6 F s son yes yes
366   O.B. White m 4 (4-25-35) F s son yes yes
367   Unknown f 1 (1-?-38) F s dau yes yes

Collier Co.
368   Frank m 23 F m Head yes yes
369   Ruby f 21 F m wife yes yes
370   Ot-to-lee m 4 (7-21-35) F s son yes yes
371   (Blank) f 2 (10-6-37) F s dau yes yes

Hendry Co.
372   George m 65 F m Head yes yes
373   Ruby f 48 F m wife yes yes
374   Wm. Buck m 11 F s son yes yes

Hendry Co.
375   Harjo m 27 F m Head yes yes
376   Mec-ta-he-thee f 16 F m wife yes yes

Hendry Co.
377   Henry m 24 F m Head yes yes
378   Betty Mae f 24 F m wife yes yes

Collier Co.
379   Ida f 60 F m Head yes yes
380   John Byrd m 13 F s grnd-son yes yes
381   Henry Byrd m 10 F s grnd-son yes yes

Collier Co.
382   Jack m 23 F m Head yes yes

KEY: Family's Resident County, (State of Florida, unless otherwise stated) Census Number
Name Sex Age at Last Birthday Tribe (Seminole, unless otherwise stated) Degree of Blood
Marital Status Relationship to Head of Family At Jurisdiction where enrolled [Yes or No] (If no,
Where) Resident County (State of Florida, unless otherwise stated) Ward [Yes or No].

383   Mary f 20 F m wife yes yes
384   Mary f 10/12 (2-16-39) F s dau yes yes

Collier Co.
385   Jimmie m 88 F w Head yes yes
386   Stoneman m 15 F s son yes yes
387   Billie m 14 F s son yes yes

Dade Co.
388   Jimmie Druitt m 42 F m Head yes yes
389   Che-si-kee f 39 F m wife yes yes
390   Unknown m 18 F s son yes yes
391   Maz Bill m 10 F s son yes yes
392   Unknown m 7 F s son yes yes
393   Unknown f 6 (10-1-33) F s dau yes yes
394   Unknown f 1 (9-13-38) F s dau yes yes

Collier Co.
395   John m 56 F m Head yes yes
396   Ar-ta-yee f 57 F m wife yes yes

Glades Co.
397   Richard m 34 (1-1-06) F m Head yes yes
398   Anna Tiger f 27 F m wife yes yes
399   Capt. Jau Don m 3 (12-20-36) F s son yes yes
400   Jimmie Scott m 2/12 (10-28-39) F s son yes yes
401   Francis m 6 (10-25-33) F s son yes yes

Glades Co.
402   Robert m 22 F m Head yes yes
403   Alice Huff f 24 F m wife yes yes
404   Bobby m 1 (3-11-38) F s son yes yes
405   **Huff, Leoda** f 7 (9-3-32) F s stp-dau yes yes
406   **Huff, Frances** f 4 (7-16-35) F s stp-dau yes yes

Hendry Co.
407   Mrs. Robert f 24 F w Head yes yes
408   Roy Nash m 9 (8-?-30) F s son yes yes

Florida Seminoles Indian Census (As of January 1, 1940)

KEY: Family's Resident County, (State of Florida, unless otherwise stated) Census Number Name Sex Age at Last Birthday Tribe (Seminole, unless otherwise stated) Degree of Blood Marital Status Relationship to Head of Family At Jurisdiction where enrolled [Yes or No] (If no, Where) Resident County (State of Florida, unless otherwise stated) Ward [Yes or No].

Dade Co.
409   Wm. McKinley m 45 F m Head yes yes
410   Ha-ta-po-kee f 38 F m wife yes yes
411   Mac m 23 F s son yes yes
412   Mittie f 21 F s dau yes yes
413   Larry m 19 F s son yes yes
414   Douglas m 16 F s son yes yes
415   Howard m 13 F s son yes yes
416   John A m 12 F s son yes yes
417   Wm. McKinley, Jr m 9 F s son yes yes
418   Agnes f 7 F s dau yes yes
419   Unknown f 1 (1-17-38) F s dau yes yes

PARKER

Glades Co.
420   Argyle m 41 F s Head yes yes

Glades Co.
421   Courtney f 46 F w Head yes yes
422   Maud f 7 (12-11-32) F s dau yes yes

Glades Co.
423   Dan m 46 F m Head yes yes
424   Tommie f 41 F m wife yes yes
425   **Jim, Little John** m 21 F s stp-son yes yes

Broward Co.
------   Mary f 17 (8-22-22) F s ? yes yes [See 516]
------   Agnes f 16 (7-22-23) F s ? yes yes [See 517]

PEARCE

Glades Co.
------   Lucy f 58 ½ W ? yes yes [See 108]
------   Ada f 29 ¾ S ? yes yes [See 109]

KEY: Family's Resident County, (State of Florida, unless otherwise stated) Census Number
Name Sex Age at Last Birthday Tribe (Seminole, unless otherwise stated) Degree of Blood
Marital Status Relationship to Head of Family At Jurisdiction where enrolled [Yes or No] (If no,
Where) Resident County (State of Florida, unless otherwise stated) Ward [Yes or No].

ROBERTS

Hendry Co.
426   Billie m 21 F s Head yes yes
427   Elsie f 22 F s sister yes yes

SHORE

Glades Co.
428   Frank m 40 F m Head yes yes
429   Lottie f 28 F m wife yes yes
430   A-ba-go-chee f 5/12 (7-5-39) F s dau yes yes

SMITH

Glades Co.
431   Dick m 59 F w Head yes yes
432   Judge Fee m 24 F s son yes yes
433   George m 12 F s son yes yes

Glades Co.
434   Jack m 18 F m Head yes yes
435   Leona Micco f 20 F m wife yes yes
436   Unknown f 4/12 (8-16-39) F s dau yes yes

Glades Co.
------ Louise f 10 F s ? yes yes [See 52]
------ Jim Stewart m 7 (10-18-32) F s ? yes yes [See 53]

Glades Co.
437   Morgan m 40 F m Head yes yes
438   Katy f 34 F m wife yes yes
439   **Jumper, Mosas** m 13 (4-16-26) F s stp-son yes yes
440   **Jumper, Lura** f 8 (11-13-31) F s stp-dau yes yes
441   Mrs. Billie f 85 F w mother yes yes
442   Dollie f 57 F s sister yes yes
443   Gullie f 42 F s sister yes yes

Florida Seminoles Indian Census (As of January 1, 1940)

KEY: Family's Resident County, (State of Florida, unless otherwise stated) Census Number Name Sex Age at Last Birthday Tribe (Seminole, unless otherwise stated) Degree of Blood Marital Status Relationship to Head of Family At Jurisdiction where enrolled [Yes or No] (If no, Where) Resident County (State of Florida, unless otherwise stated) Ward [Yes or No].

St. Lucie Co.

444 Tom m 51 F m Head yes yes
445 Stella Josh f 40 ¾ m wife yes yes
446 In-go-wa-pa f 13 7/8 s dau yes yes
447 In-sla-ba f 11 7/8 s dau yes yes
448 In-to-sli-kee f 3 (3-27-36) 7/8 s dau yes yes
449 I-yus-chee f 3 (3-27-36) 7/8 s dau yes yes
450 Mun-da-la m 2 (1937) 7/8 s son yes yes

SNOW

Glades Co.
451 Sampson m 44 F m Head yes yes
452 Ma-tha-noc-kee f 38 F m wife yes yes
453 Bob Pearce m 20 F s son yes yes
454 Sho-lee f 10 (8-1-29) F s dau yes yes
455 Josephine f 7 (4-1-32) F s dau yes yes
456 Jennie f 6 F s dau yes yes

STEWART

Glades Co.
457 Susie Tiger F 61 F w Head yes yes
458 Fannie f 38 F s dau yes yes
459 **Charlie, Big** m 57 F s brother yes yes

TIGER

Broward Co.
460 Ada f 41 F w Head yes yes
461 Betty Mae f 18 (4-7-21) ½ s dau yes yes
462 Howard m 15 (8-27-24) ½ s son yes yes
463 Mary Gopher f 80 F w mother yes yes

Hendry Co.
464 Bobbie Jim m 35 F m Head yes yes
465 Mary f 26 F m wife yes yes

Florida Seminoles Indian Census (As of January 1, 1940)

KEY: Family's Resident County, (State of Florida, unless otherwise stated) Census Number Name Sex Age at Last Birthday Tribe (Seminole, unless otherwise stated) Degree of Blood Marital Status Relationship to Head of Family At Jurisdiction where enrolled [Yes or No] (If no, Where) Resident County (State of Florida, unless otherwise stated) Ward [Yes or No].

Dade Co.
466   Brown m 49 F w Head yes yes

Collier Co.
467   Charlie m 63 F w Head yes yes

Collier Co.
468   Doctor m 87 F w Head yes yes

Hendry Co.
469   Cuffney m 72 F m Head yes yes
470   Ma-fo-lo-tee f 56 F m wife yes yes

Collier Co.
471   Emma f 49 F w Head yes yes
472   Pauline Poole f 24 F s dau yes yes

Collier Co.
473   Frank m 49 F w Head yes yes
474   Mary f 23 F s dau yes yes
475   Henry m 21 F s son yes yes
476   Dorothy f 4 (8-12-35) F s grnd-dau yes yes

Collier Co.
477   John Frank m 31 F m Head yes yes
478   Annie f 23 F m wife yes yes

Collier Co.
479   John Poole m 28 F m Head yes yes
480   Camilla f 22 F m wife yes yes
481   Unknown f ? (12-4-39) F s dau yes yes

Hendry Co.
482   Little m 37 F m Head yes yes
483   Shee-ma-ho-thee f 30 F m wife yes yes
484   Toc-shee f 4 (8-14-35) F s dau yes yes
485   Unknown m 2 (4-?-37) F s son yes yes
486   Harriett f 6/12 (6-26-39) F s dau yes yes

Florida Seminoles Indian Census (As of January 1, 1940)

KEY: **Family's Resident County**, (State of Florida, unless otherwise stated) Census Number Name Sex Age at Last Birthday Tribe (Seminole, unless otherwise stated) Degree of Blood Marital Status Relationship to Head of Family At Jurisdiction where enrolled [Yes or No] (If no, Where) Resident County (State of Florida, unless otherwise stated) Ward [Yes or No].

Glades Co.
487   Na-ha   m   54   F   m   Head   yes   yes
488   Lucy   f   62   F   m   wife   yes   yes

Collier Co.
489   Tiger   m   45   F   m   Head   yes   yes
490   Ruby   f   42   F   m   wife   yes   yes
491   Frank   m   21   F   s   son   yes   yes
492   Cypress   m   17   F   s   son   yes   yes
493   Harjo   m   14   F   s   son   yes   yes
494   Ar-we-che-hen-ee   f   11 (2-18-28)   F   s   dau   yes   yes
495   O-yan-ho-yee   f   9   F   s   dau   yes   yes

Collier Co.
496   Tiger Boy [Jimmie]   m   25   F   m   Head   yes   yes
497   Martha   f   22   F   m   wife   yes   yes
498   Lum-hee   m   4 (9-20-35)   F   s   son   yes   yes

Collier Co.
499   Willie   m   75   F   w   Head   yes   yes

Collier Co.
500   Willie   m   20 (1920)   F   m   Head   yes   yes
501   Maggie   f   17   F   m   wife   yes   yes
502   Unknown   f   1 (12-31-38)   F   s   dau   yes   yes
503   Flora   f   21 (11-1-18)   F   s   sister   yes   yes
504   Unknown   f   1 (3-9-38)   F   s   niece   yes   yes

TIGERTAIL

Glades Co.
------   Frances   f   9   F   s   ?   yes   yes   [See 93]

Dade Co.
505   John White   m   25   F   s   Head   yes   yes
506   Lena   f   24   F   s   sister   yes   yes
507   Frances   f   19   F   s   sister   yes   yes

Florida Seminoles Indian Census (As of January 1, 1940)

KEY: **Family's Resident County**, (State of Florida, unless otherwise stated) Census Number Name Sex Age at Last Birthday Tribe (Seminole, unless otherwise stated) Degree of Blood Marital Status Relationship to Head of Family At Jurisdiction where enrolled [Yes or No] (If no, Where) Resident County (State of Florida, unless otherwise stated) Ward [Yes or No].

Hendry Co.

508   Kat-ath-lee [Little] m 24 F m Head yes yes
509   Belle f 27 F m wife yes yes

TOMMIE

Broward Co.

510   Annie f 84 F w Head yes yes
511   Annie Mae f 46 F s dau yes yes
512   Brownie m 41 F s son yes yes

Broward Co.

513   Ben m 57 F m Head yes yes
514   Tudie f 45 F m wife yes yes
515   Mary f 18 (6-17-21) F s dau yes yes
516   **Parker, Mary** f 17 (8-22-22) F s niece yes yes
517   **Parker, Agnes** f 16 (7-22-23) F s niece yes yes

Broward Co.

518   Frank m 44 F m Head yes yes
519   Sadie f 34 F m wife yes yes
520   Willie Micco m 13 F s son yes yes
521   O-Kay m 10 F s son yes yes

Glades Co.

522   Jack m 44 F m Head yes yes
523   Sally f 35 F m wife yes yes
524   Cleveland m 21 F s son yes yes
525   Rosa Lee f 19 (8-19-20) F s dau yes yes
526   George m 18 F s son yes yes
527   Fred Smith m 16 F s son yes yes
528   Ada H f 13 F s dau yes yes
529   Setie Buck m 11 (8-12-28) F s son yes yes
530   Walter Shine m 9 F s son yes yes
531   Minnie f 6 F s dau yes yes
532   Hope f 3 (11-1-36) F s dau yes yes
533   Unknown f 10/12 (2-4-39) F s dau yes yes

Florida Seminoles Indian Census (As of January 1, 1940)

KEY: **Family's Resident County**, (State of Florida, unless otherwise stated) Census Number Name Sex Age at Last Birthday Tribe (Seminole, unless otherwise stated) Degree of Blood Marital Status Relationship to Head of Family At Jurisdiction where enrolled [Yes or No] (If no, Where) Resident County (State of Florida, unless otherwise stated) Ward [Yes or No].

Dade Co.
534   Jimmie m 43 F m Head yes yes
535   Lobee f 36 F m wife yes yes
536   Billie m 13 F s son yes yes
537   Jimmie m 10 F s son yes yes
538   As-sa-po-ha-tee f 6 (10-19-33) F s dau yes yes
539   Nok-co-chee f 1 (8-2-38) F s dau yes yes

Collier Co.
540   Noki [Lady] f 36 F w Head yes yes
541   Baby Morgan f 16 F s dau yes yes

Palm Beach Co.
542   Sam m 35 F m Head yes yes
543   Mary f 26 F m wife yes yes
544   Harry m 9 F s son yes yes
545   Sadie f 7 (10-1-32) F s dau yes yes
546   Sally f 3 (5-24-36) F s dau yes yes
547   Unknown m 1 (5-29-38) F s son yes yes

Collier Co.
548   Small-pox m 53 F m Head yes yes
549   Mary f 45 F m wife yes yes

TONY

Collier Co.
550   Fi-yic-chee (Mrs. Capt. Young) f 52 F w Head yes yes
551   Martha f 27 F s dau yes yes

TUCKER

St. Lucie Co.
552   Chaw-huc-kee f 78 F w Head yes yes
553   Susie f 62 F s dau yes yes
554   Mait-kah f 59 F s dau yes yes
555   Sar-thler-na-kee f 36 F s dau yes yes

KEY: **Family's Resident County**, (State of Florida, unless otherwise stated) Census Number
Name Sex Age at Last Birthday Tribe (Seminole, unless otherwise stated) Degree of Blood
Marital Status Relationship to Head of Family At Jurisdiction where enrolled [Yes or No] (If no,
Where) Resident County (State of Florida, unless otherwise stated) Ward [Yes or No].

Collier Co.

556	Frank	m	34	F	m	Head	yes	yes
557	Mary	f	30	F	m	wife	yes	yes
558	Frank McGill	m	10	F	s	son	yes	yes
559	Sho-no-see	m	5 (11-?-34)	F	s	son	yes	yes
560	Shepak-kee	f	3 (5-7-36)	F	s	dau	yes	yes
561	A-no-ke	m	1 (9-12-38)	F	s	son	yes	yes

Glades Co.

------ Lewis m 51 ½ s ? yes yes [See 107]

WELLS

Glades Co.

562 Ben m 31 F s Head yes yes

WILLIE

Dade Co.

563	Frank	m	55	F	m	Head	yes	yes
564	Ba-shee	f	33	F	m	wife	yes	yes
565	Ya-pa-te-he-nee	f	21	F	s	dau	yes	yes
566	**Charlie, Pauline**	f	21	F	s	stp-dau	yes	yes

Dade Co.

567	Henry Sam	m	21	F	m	Head	yes	yes
568	Mickie	f	23	F	m	wife	yes	yes
569	Galvin	m	3 (8-25-38)	F	s	son	yes	yes
570	Unknown	m	1 (6-30-38)	F	s	son	yes	yes

Dade Co.

571	Jessie	m	40	F	m	Head	yes	yes
572	Lic-chee	f	37	F	m	wife	yes	yes
573	Fi-kee	f	20	F	s	dau	yes	yes
574	Tom-me-sa-chee	f	19	F	s	dau	yes	yes
575	Sac-he-pee	f	6	F	s	dau	yes	yes
576	Unknown	f	4	F	s	dau	yes	yes

Florida Seminoles Indian Census (As of January 1, 1940)

KEY: Family's Resident County, (State of Florida, unless otherwise stated) Census Number Name Sex Age at Last Birthday Tribe (Seminole, unless otherwise stated) Degree of Blood Marital Status Relationship to Head of Family At Jurisdiction where enrolled [Yes or No] (If no, Where) Resident County (State of Florida, unless otherwise stated) Ward [Yes or No].

Dade Co.
577   Johnny m 77 F w Head yes yes

Collier Co.
------   Ruby f 49 F w ? yes yes [See 102]
------   Little m 10 (1-15-29) F s ? yes yes [See 103]

Dade Co.
578   Sam m 48 F m Head yes yes
579   She-mo-ka-tee f 40 F m wife yes yes
580   Walter Roy m 18 F s son yes yes
581   Ruby f 19 F s dau yes yes
582   Be-kol-ha-chee m 13 F s son yes yes

Dade Co.
583   Sam Frank m 24 F m Head yes yes
584   Fi-ne-chee f 24 F m wife yes yes
585   Unknown m 10 F s son yes yes
586   Unknown f 3 (?) F s dau yes yes

191

www.ingramcontent.com/pod-product-compliance
Lightning Source LLC
Chambersburg PA
CBHW030304030426
42336CB00009B/513